"Sit comfortably but straight
shoulders down but not
hunched, elbows in, arms
hanging level with the
keyboard, wrists somewhat
higher so that the hands hang
slightly when the fingers
push down the keys."

Photos courtesy of Servicio Grafico International.

MUSIC AT YOUR FINGERTIPS

By Ruth Slenczynska

WITH THE COLLABORATION OF

Ann M. Lingg

MUSIC AT YOUR FINGERTIPS

Doubleday & Company, Inc.
Garden City, New York
1961

To Sister Mary de Chantal

CONTENTS

Whatever we know and believe we have learned through the perception of our senses, psychologists tell us. The intensity of each sense varies with the individual. Some of us are dominated by sight perception; others receive their strongest impressions through the ear or by kinesthetic absorption. Modern education might tend to dull the subtle variety of sensory reaction that exists in every child's potential. Perhaps it is the early application of undulled sensory perception to outside stimuli that creates a child prodigy; later education can either "educate away" the child's untutored acuteness of reaction or stimulate certain traits that will develop into artistic individuality. Many of the recommendations on practice methods given here may seem general and overly simple; yet they are the net result of thirty years of learning, experience, thoroughly digested, mulled over, applied during years of teaching at every level, and again polished and broadened for a revived and extremely active concert career. I am not repeating to you, like a parrot, the many little things about specific problems that my own teachers taught me, but rather the principles behind them. I have kept perfecting the foundation that was mine at fourteen, in years of experience, until I have acquired a set of tools that may be useful to others who pursue the same pianistic goal.

First and foremost, I was taught to listen (as distinguished from "hearing") and to learn from all sources with an open, credulous, and investigating mind and with the determination to make a piece "sound right," regardless of the means required to achieve this end.

In 1929, when I was four, I had some lessons with a Leschetizky pupil, Mrs. Alma Schmidt-Kennedy. After every lesson, she delighted me with a story from Greek mythology. This opened to me the world of images and imagination, made me understand the connection between imagery and music, and implanted in me the idea that a good musician is interested in many different things for their own sake.

In 1929 I also met Josef Hofmann, of the Curtis Institute, and a year later I had a few lessons with him. Five years after that we happened to cross the Atlantic on the same boat. During our week aboard the S.S. *Washington* he spent practically all his free time with me and instilled in me the idea that even technical problems are controlled by the mind. I came to realize that sufficient mental effort produces a satisfactory solution, whatever the difficulty.

In 1930–31 I worked under Egon Petri, who combined a disconcerting contradiction of magnificent technical ability with excessive modesty in his speech. He taught me many important technical expediencies. He thought in terms of "I'll try my very best and hope it will come out well," which is dangerous for a youngster because often the very best he can do doesn't come out well at all. I became unhappy to the point of self-despisement and

didn't regain confidence until 1934, when I had Rachmaninoff to guide me. "Who are you?" he would say.
"You're only a child. Why should your best be good
enough? Don't look into a mirror; look at the music!"

In 1931–32 I studied Beethoven, Bach, Schubert,
and Mozart with Artur Schnabel, who imported enormous
relaxation and assuredness through his inflexible, literal
interpretation. Every one of his performances followed
an unchanging master plan, even though he was free
within his own boundaries. No other pianist, then or now,
thought quite in this manner—perhaps a lost art.

Alfred Cortot, with whom I worked from 1932 for
seven years, was just the opposite. He taught me to
improvise. "Music is poetry. Once you have played, it's
over. You can never express the same thing twice in the
same way."

I had many other teachers, some of them less famous.
My father supervised my studies from infancy. For three
years I took lessons from Marguerite Long, who made
me supersensitive to the timber of every note. For two
seasons I worked with Lazare Lévy, a genius for inventive
fingering.

Isidor Philipp gave me books of his finger exercises,
and those of Brahms. Nadia Boulanger taught me harmony, mainly by having me analyze Bach's chorales.
My family and I lived in Europe most of the time; in
1939, after the war forced us to return home for good,
Dr. Albert Elkus, then heading the Music Department
of the University of California, kindled my interest in
books on music; I began to study the lives of the great

composers and to explore the music libraries, which I still do.

In this book I am not meting out musical advice; rather I discuss practice method. For the student the main psychological advantage of taking lessons is the stimulus from an outside source he respects, until such time as he can find the stimulus within himself. Every great artist once started as a student who gradually assimilated his own concepts, tested methods and musical thoughts, learned from false start and failure as well as from success, developed his musical personality through knowledge, hard work, and optimism. The most celebrated virtuoso and the most inexperienced student work with the same raw material, the printed score, the only true authority. All the teacher can do is to give the budding musician a reliable set of tools and to spark the love for music and the desire to communicate.

MUSIC AT YOUR FINGERTIPS

CHAPTER ONE

Personality Factors

WHAT MAKES a composition a work of art? What is the special quality that starts a chain of inspirations that stay with the listener and stimulate creative thought of his own? A Beethoven symphony has remained popular through one and a half centuries, fresh through thousands of performances, because its creative fire continues to kindle the imagination, to stir emotion in all of us. It is impossible to miss the spirit of genuine art. If, before an audience, we could fashion a proud, lovely rose, arrange each leaf, each petal until it is perfect, and then make it live even for an instant, it would be an unforgettable experience for all who watched. This is what must happen when we re-create music, when we make a composition live for a few minutes, for half an hour; the quality of living force must be there if our re-creation is to be meaningful.

Being human, we musicians can reflect only what we are, as in a mirror. Any affectation, the slightest insincerity, instantly reveals itself as sham.

We receive sparks of inspiration, store them carefully

in our memories, and, when released, they fire our own re-creative power. I can relive the thrill I felt as a small child at Joseph Lhévinne's playing of *La Campanella* by Paganini-Liszt, at Ignaz Friedman's interpretation of Chopin's "Étude in Thirds," at Rachmaninoff's magical rendition of his Third Concerto, at the rich velvet tone of Mischa Elman's Concerto of Bruch. These are supreme moments in our lives because they affirm that we humble humans have the power to re-create living beauty.

By strong discipline, thorough training, broad and bold musical conceptions we can capture this power to re-create.

Many personality factors go into the making of an artist: a high degree of imagination, intelligence, sensitivity, flexibility; the willingness to learn from every situation, to plod doggedly even when the going gets rugged; the courage of our artistic convictions even when fashionable musical opinion makers leave us in the minority. We must be stubborn optimists who will spend hours, weeks, even months working on dull problems of technique. Sometimes faith is the only thing to carry us over a veritable chasm of despair. Those of us who are inclined to daydream should train themselves to plod; those who plod too hard and dream too little should force themselves to relax and let their imagination roam freely. In a performance heart, mind, and hands all work together. The heart is filled to overflowing with wonder and beauty; the mind learns how to communicate these emotions; the hands must obediently, and under all conditions, execute the musical ideas that heart and mind command.

When we plant a seed to grow a flower we know its name, its color, shape, and approximate size at full bloom. We see it in our mind's eye taking its place in the garden setting we have chosen for it. Music-making isn't much different. We must be able to imagine every tone, every phrase, the whole composition as we wish it to sound, all the way to the grand sweep of the entire work, and we must be able to project it so that the listener receives precisely the impression we wish to create.

The rose you have planted in your garden will be beautiful any time of day—in the early light of dawn, in the bright sun of noontime, in the blush of sunset, in the white light of the full moon. Likewise, in music, your re-creation must always be convincing whether played on a spinet, a baby grand, a concert grand; whether in a living room, a small theater, a huge gymnasium, or outdoors.

We can even accept our own limitations and still be artists as long as we make the most of our possibilities from the very start. In art everything is worth while; art is luxury of the spirit. The smallest accomplishment is at least self-fulfilling and adds to our understanding of music and its beauty. Music is an integral part of living; a part of the air we breathe, a language more full of meaning than any spoken tongue. Communicative performance is the glorious beacon that can make even humdrum practicing a joy.

CHAPTER TWO

Music Is a Language

MUSIC IS a living language, more eloquent than any spoken tongue. The performer is the translator, the interpreter.

From the first note at our first lesson, all through our musical lives, we must aim at making every sound meaningful.

Most pianists play by ear. We never hear exactly how the music sounds as we play. We sit in front of the keyboard and the sound emerges about four feet down, to the right of the open piano wing. This is the spot toward which we should project our tone, where we should place ourselves as imaginary listeners. Franz Liszt once said that you must listen to yourself as critically as if you were a rival pianist in another room. Pianists often are so preoccupied with producing music that they forget about receiving it; this is why, to criticize constructively, we must imagine ourselves away from the piano and concentrate on the continuous, meaningful flow of the musical line.

I like to practice with the piano fully open and the music rack down in order to give myself a feeling of space.

In performance, when the piano wing is up to reflect the tone into the auditorium, I look through the open piano and find a place on which to concentrate my gaze. I imagine myself right there, listening. When I play with an orchestra, I usually play to one of the faces in the second-violin section. I try to express the subtlest nuance in every tone, to project it toward myself as audience. Once this becomes a habit, it will not be difficult to project toward a real audience of two thousand or twenty thousand, in a drawing room, an auditorium, before a microphone. Wherever we are we play for some definite listener at a definite place—ourselves—near the open wing of the piano.

Mischa Elman, the violin virtuoso, feels that it is more important for the pianist than any other instrumentalist to practice the art of the uninterrupted melodic line. This is easier for singers and string players because they normally work with only one melody, while keyboard artists have a host of other factors to consider: two performing hands, two assisting feet, the problem of keeping the melody free from interference by harmonies and pedals. Sometimes it is a real effort to free a melody, to make it sing flowingly and shape its musical line in one big sweep from beginning to end. Play your musical phrase and give your fullest, uninterrupted attention to the musical line. Be careful never to exaggerate the accent at the peak of the phrase or to let it get lost between a crescendo and a diminuendo; the musical line must flow naturally.

To establish the mood of a phrase, to blend it with

its setting, to convey what we believe to be the precise meaning the composer wishes to express, is one of the greatest problems facing a pianist and one of the most thrilling adventures in a day's work. I have said that the language of music is the most eloquent of all, but it is also the most elusive, working by innuendo only, suggesting rather than stating, sometimes confusing us as to the composer's real intentions.

Here is a device that should be equally helpful to the beginner learning a Haydn minuet and the virtuoso reading, say, a Liszt rhapsody for the first time: use the spoken word as a spark plug. Isolate the musical phrase, then tell yourself audibly, in plain language, what you think it was meant to express. Joy? Grief? Or homesickness, complaint, pain, gaiety, passion, foreboding? After you have decided on the most fitting verbal expression, experiment at the piano until you succeed in establishing the mood musically. You will soon be able to convey the basic meaning, as you feel it, in musical terms; then develop it in every possible way. The melody sings forth imperturbably, but harmonies and the cautious use of the pedal assist you.

I remember how Rachmaninoff explained to me the problem of phrasing: he showed me an elastic band and stretched it slightly, then allowed it to bounce back; next, he stretched it beyond a certain point, and it snapped. He meant to say that no part of a musical line should be stretched out of proportion to the whole composition. We have a natural tendency to take a breath, so to speak, after each phrase, but we must be careful not to overdo it. Actually the end of one phrase should prepare the listener for the next, or at least blend into it so that the musical fabric remains strong and whole. There are even instances in which a whole series of phrases leads up to a sort of gateway opening a new mood; almost as if another light had been turned on—for example, the E♭ major chord in Measure 21 of the second movement of Chopin's F minor Concerto.

This brings us to the very stringent problem of diminuendo: for some reason it tempts us to slow down, but diminuendo only means diminished sonority and must not interfere with the rhythmic pulse of the music. A pianist who reduces tempo together with volume is either a beginner or a bad musician. Chopin felt so strongly about this that he recommended always to practice with the metronome.

Whatever the tone volume, a ritardando must be smooth, almost imperceptible. Casals compared it to an automobile stopping at a red light: "If you stop abruptly, you fall forward and break your skull. Slow down gradually so that everything remains in place and you can get out of your car with dignity." Ritardandi must be as gentle as possible. Only the pianist must know that they are there at all.

Usually, as we grow older, the relationship to our repertoire matures; our ideas of what a particular phrase, a particular composition should express become more complex. Let's take the opening theme of the last movement of Chopin's F minor Concerto, which Huneker called "Mazurka-like, very graceful, and full of pure sweet melody."

When I first learned it I was about twelve years old. I played it in its most straightforward manner, with simple peasant gaiety. A few years later I gave it more polish and put the gaiety in a more elegant setting; I had come to feel in it echoes of the aristocracy of Chopin and his Parisian audiences. For many concerts this seemed to me the correct interpretation. Then, after a period of years, I discovered a note of complaint that changed the character of the gay theme and gave it a new element of drama. This was a fascinating process I experienced many times. As we grow with a musical work we constantly seek and find new nuances, new details, new meanings, and whatever we accepted in the past appears as a mere half-truth to which we can never return.

I never make notes in my scores. I like to start afresh at every relearning. Perhaps some minute detail not noticed before or not fully understood will give an entirely new meaning to a phrase.

Creation is alive, so re-creation must also be alive. Life is movement. Clouds float, leaves stir in the breeze. Our organs, our glands, are in motion even while we sleep; the moment they stop we are dead. A brook that stops flowing becomes a stagnant pool. A melody without direction becomes purposeless.

Most great music was written according to definite architectural lines; each small detail has its place, from the first sound to the last.

When we examine a phrase we see many things in it

as a phrase unit. When we combine it with the next phrase, its connotation changes completely, for we are looking at a two-phrase unit. Longer compositions should be divided into sections as long as possible, so that each phrase receives correct dimensions.

Every section is a musical paragraph like a prose paragraph the meaning of which can usually be summed up in a few words. Each has a point toward which the music builds and from which it recedes. Some music builds all the way to the last note, i.e., the Fugue from Bach's *Chromatic Fantasy and Fugue*. Mostly, however, melody moves like the ebb and flow of an ocean tide; many small waves help build up to a mighty climax, then subside again and become absorbed by the expanse of rolling water. See, for example, Chopin's Étude, Opus 10, No. 3, in E major.

But there is also miniature music, intimate music. Here a tiny dynamic scale and phrase are in order, with a view to daintiness rather than grandeur. Again, we must look for the direction of the basic melody, for the climax of each section, each phrase. Every detail has to fit into its setting. A *sfz* in a Schubert waltz is an entirely different *sfz* from that in a Brahms concerto.

To sum up, here are three basic rules:

1. Concentrate for the full length of the musical line, without interruption.

2. Determine the mood to be expressed and make every detail point toward it.

3. Find the focal point or climax of a phrase or section in order to give direction to your musical thought.

Beauty of sound is another pianistic virtue that must be acquired from the very start. The great composers for the keyboard placed much emphasis on the quality of tone. Debussy gave a rather sweeping order: "Every sound must be beautiful." Chopin insisted that one should always practice on the best piano available and keep it in perfect tune to accustom the ear to the finest possible sound.

Even when we practice scales our sound can be beautiful. We must never forget the infinite variety of tonal shading we are able to produce, the variations of touch, of which there are thousands. The shaping and mixing of sound are our most personal contribution to the re-creative process. "Nuances are the musician's palette," said Liszt. "His hand must master them completely, so they are at his beck and call." Like nothing else, they reveal the pianist's personality.

Even a child learning his first piece can be helped to project personality. I suggest to let him sing the melody away from the piano; if this is difficult at first, the teacher might block it out on paper, illustrate the phrase as exactly as possible, indicate where to sing loudly or softly, where to place an accent, where to grow or diminish. As the child first learns by imitation, he will lose his inhibitions, and suddenly his own reactions will come flooding into the little piece of music, young as he might be. He will learn the naturalness of the rise and fall of a phrase because he will have to breathe as he

sings; then at the piano he will simply transfer what he
has learned and the melody will come alive.

Always a student must be admonished to make technical exercises sound beautiful: to use crescendo and diminuendo, to listen to his sound, to polish his tones, to aim
at an even quality. At first the tonal palette will be mea-
ger, even crude; new students tend to use either *pp* or *ff*
just as the novice painter works at first only with the
primary colors. Normally the pianist's first showpiece gets
the biggest acclaim when played in the *f* to *ff* range, so
that end of the dynamic scale is usually explored first.
(As Moriz Rosenthal once quipped, "As long as you've
got to play the piano, do it loud and fast.")

Then someone may tactfully suggest that the pupil
is playing too forcefully, at which he may flee to the
opposite end of the dynamic scale and explore *pp* to *p*.
It takes a while to come to terms with the many variations
of touch and sound in between.

Once as a child I played a Chopin nocturne for
Alfred Cortot. He said, "This was no good, and you know
it. Play it again as if you were the teacher showing me
how to play." I played it again and he was satisfied. This
taught me a most important lesson. It was the beginning
of my campaign for what I call "exercises in imagination."

Through exercises in imagination the novice will
learn variety of touch.

Instead of telling him merely, "Play louder," or "Play
softer," I tell him "Sound happier," or "Try a melancholy
undertone." Instead of saying "Put more forearm strength

2

25

into this note," I might tell him to put more warmth of feeling into the passage. Everybody has a different physical solution to a given tonal problem, depending on the size and strength of hands and arms, and on previous experience.

I make sure that the student avoids muscular tenseness and watch out for weak spots in his technique to be repaired by appropriate exercises; otherwise I let him find his own physical solution, almost like the boy Mozart, who once used his nose to push down a key in a chord he could not span.

With exercises in imagination the pupil stops playing mere notes; he is making music, his sounds conveying meaning to the listener. When a small child learns his first gavotte, minuet, waltz, the teacher might take him by the hand, lead him off the piano bench into the room, and have him *dance* to the music so that he *feels* what he is trying to express. Once a child experiences this freedom of movement, he can transfer it to the music, just as he transferred to the keyboard his first experience of singing a melodic line.

A child's dormant imagination might go to waste unless developed by the teacher. By feeling and doing small things, imaginative powers can eventually face enormous projects. Debussy wrote *La Mer* without ever having seen the ocean, but he knew what the feeling of the ocean must be and he could express it in music because he had previously written other, smaller tone pictures communicating impressions received.

CHAPTER THREE

Concepts of Proportion, Tempo, Rhythm

To CREATE and sustain a mood is a fragile procedure —the net that casts the spell, that holds the audience. Without "mood" the finest performance remains but a reproduction of notes, black-and-white sound pictures untouched by human warmth, that may command respect but will never capture the imagination. It is the adventure of the unknown, the vast imponderable area created by the questions whether we have chosen the right mood for our interpretation, and how we communicate it to the audience, that supplies the personal touch, makes a concert interesting, exciting, alive.

The art of re-creation is full of seeming contradictions. A performance must sound fresh and spontaneous, almost improvised; yet every tone, every nuance, the slightest pause, the most furtive slur, must be the result of careful, endless study and experimentation.

Every masterpiece is based on an architectural plan. This is its steel skeleton into which we fill the mass of detail, inflection, accent. We don't always fill it in quite the same manner. We practice in order to develop flexibility, sensitivity, maximum mastery of our instrument. But also, practice gives us the only sure footing in a sea of imponderables.

✓ [Rhythm is the basic pulse of a composition;] tempo, its pace. A steady rhythmic pulse can be developed with hard practice, but tempo remains arbitrary. We have no proper vocabulary to indicate exact rates of speed, beyond such generalities as *largo* (broad), *andante* (walking), *vivace* (lively), *allegro* (happy), *presto* (fast), *grave* (serious), and many more, most of which are indicative of mood rather than of motion. No two artists use precisely the same tempo in a given composition; hardly any artist uses precisely the same tempo every time he plays the same piece. Actually it may vary slightly from piano to piano because, to maintain the proper mood, we must exploit the possibilities of every instrument to best advantage.

A student's *presto*, for example, may sound very fast because he will play as fast as he can manage and his efforts to hurry become evident; but when an artist uses the same tempo it might sound slow, since he has perfect control of his hands and *sounds* controlled, while the student *sounds* hurried. This is why I recommend use of the metronome from the very beginning, from the very first scale, throughout our musical lives. I still use it daily, even on tour, to maintain the discipline of daily practice and full mastery of the keyboard, even when the keyboards vary. The best kind is the pocket-watch metronome because it can be carried anywhere, sounds soft enough not to distract, and is built so that one can more accurately regulate the rate at which to increase the speed.

Proportion is the elusive cousin of architecture. It is one of the most difficult, and one of the basic, problems of a pianist. Tempo, rhythm, dynamics, mood—all these elements must have been explored before we can hope to attain the ideal proportion. We can establish the "right" tempo only if we realize what would be too fast or too slow. We arrive at controlled tone color only if we know what is too loud or too soft. Exaggeration and understatement, constant probing of detail, alone will teach us to project all shades of mood.

First, we must know how to approach a passage technically. Just as we wear different kinds of coats for different kinds of weather, we use a different technique for every mood. Cortot recommends a light, quick, almost staccato fingertip touch for passages of rapid fingerwork, and a flat, ball-of-the-finger caress of the keys for slow legato. There are a thousand secrets of touch that a pianist's ear can teach.

Robert Schumann felt that the cultivation of the ear was of prime importance. In his "House Rules and Maxims for Young Musicians" he tells them to endeavor in good time to listen to the sounds around them—the doorbell, the windowpane, the cuckoo—and to discover which tones and key they produce. Every piano requires a slightly different touch; every room in which we play requires different volume.

Chopin practiced a great deal of Mozart and Bach during his formative years to acquire a sensitive touch.

29

Mozart sonatas are ideal to develop the *p* to *mp* to *mf* to *f* area of dynamics. Bach's original works for keyboard, especially the fugues, are the best conditioners for hands and mind, and I suggest devoting one hour daily to their practice; they teach us finger control so we can play many voices at once, keeping them separate, clear, and expressive, yet within the fabric of the whole composition; this background in polyphonic thinking will always be useful. Rachmaninoff recommended Scarlatti as an invigorating "cold bath" for finger technique. After I had had a ten-day vacation from the piano—he put me on an exclusive diet of Scarlatti sonatas for three weeks in order to recondition my touch.

Franz Liszt had a method of practicing that is worth noting because it was the foundation for the revolutionary technique that established him as the "father of modern pianism." He was not yet twenty, living in Paris, when he was overawed by Paganini's phenomenal virtuosity and pledged himself to achieve on the keyboard what this man achieved on four strings. He developed his method by himself and submitted himself to a merciless drill of his fingers six hours a day:

Octaves in scales for two hours to make his fingers both strong and supple; he lifted his hands high and attacked the keys with full energy. The same for chords and arpeggios.

Repetition of notes, octaves, and chords on the same key for muscular control; trills, with the other three fingers resting on the keys.

He was careful not to move arms and shoulders, or to

bend his head forward; he sat straight and bent his head backward, but very little.

New pieces were studied in five stages. He started by reading very slowly, four or five times, each time from a different angle. First only the notes; secondly, note values; thirdly, nuances, changes in expression; fourthly, analyzing bass and descant, always searching for melodies that could be accentuated; finally he decided on the tempi. Then he began to practice: he analyzed his own emotional reactions and, after passionate passages, would proceed as if indifferent or tired to express the natural slackening of feeling after an emotional storm. He insisted that passionate self-abandon to the music had to dictate a pianist's interpretation, but he had to have perfect physical control of his hands. "Never must your fingers stand in the way of your artistic interpretation," Carl Czerny, his own teacher, had always said to him.

When I study a new piece, I start to practice very slowly with the metronome to get it comfortably and accurately into my fingers; and I play it slowly until I have the feeling of perfect control. Forcing speed too soon is like forcing a child to walk before he is ready. You accomplish no progress, and you can jeopardize the equilibrium and control you may have acquired.

In my steadily growing repertoire I find that every piece of music has its price, in terms of effort to get it under control. There is no passage so difficult that it would not be possible to find a metronome speed slow enough to play it comfortably. We must train the mind before we train our hands; and the mind first balks at adding new patterns to its subconscious; so we have to placate it, cajole it, prove that the new pattern can be easy—which we achieve by working at a slow tempo. Once the composition is acquired, our memory will retain it, and we have plenty of time to play it as fast as we want.

Once I know a passage thoroughly at a slow tempo, I take it a little faster, mostly only two metronome numbers, so that the mind and the hands hardly notice the change. At each playing I increase the speed by two metronome numbers until I reach a limit where I can still deliver the passage accurately but can't exceed that speed. There I stop.

At the next practice period I start all over again from the original slow tempo, which already seems considerably easier than a few hours before. If it feels very much easier, I advance at the rate of three metronome numbers, guarding, however, that the fingers don't feel the strain. I never go beyond the point of tension; this point advances by itself, day by day, week by week, without forcing, until I reach a point far beyond the speed I need. Yet, I still start slowly every day and never exceed a five number advancement rate, because the muscles would feel the strain and the foundations of the kinesthetic response that I am trying to build might be shaken. At times this way of practicing seems monotonous, but I have found that the time spent is well invested. Incidentally, I learned it from Rachmaninoff, who felt that it was the only way to gain firm fingers.

Sometimes it happens to me, as to every pianist, that

I hit a snag with some difficult passage. Then I simply put it away for some time. When I revive it I am sometimes amazed to see to what degree my earlier work bears fruit. The piece suddenly seems easier, my playing surer, more accurate. It is as if it had been germinating all by itself.

I have given considerable thought to the pros and cons of metronome drill; that is, to the extent to which it should be used:

I have found that it gives best results when done every day. It is useful not only to maintain rhythm, but also for fingerwork, octave work, jump passages, even memorizing, for it relieves the mind of the mechanical chore of counting rhythm. I am a slow memorizer and have experimented with different procedures, none of them as effective in the long run. The different speeds force us to hear the same passages in many different ways, thus helping us to free it from the printed paper and fixing every tiny detail in our minds. Daily we become stronger as we work from beginning to end, from slow to almost concert tempo, improving our mental and technical grasp, always smoothing away rough spots. On really complicated, stubborn passages I practice three times at each metronome speed, in the following manner:

(1) right hand *f* with left hand *p*
(2) left hand *f* with right hand *p*
(3) both hands in proper proportion

I have yet to find a problem that could not be solved, partly at least, by metronome drill.

I always aim at a faster tempo than I will need. In performance it should never be necessary to use your ability to the limits; there should always be a margin of reserve. Here again, one of Rachmaninoff's truisms: "If you want a horse to run a mile-long race, train him to run a mile and a half; then the mile will be easy."

On the other hand, the metronome is only a means to an end, a tool. It should never be considered more than that. While it helps us to gain freedom from technical problems and to acquire the "margin of reserve," we have to learn in good time to acquire freedom from the metronome itself. To me the metronome is like the chrysalis that protects the insect until it has grown into a butterfly. We must use the metronome to good advantage but not become its prisoner.

First there was freedom from technical problems, then freedom from the metronome; finally there is freedom from the keyboard, so essential for technical assuredness as well as beautiful tone. If our hands are "glued" to the keyboard, afraid of losing notes or hand position, our tone will become monotonous and sound as unfree as we actually are. In order to free your hands I suggest making exercises of such compositions as the following:

Bach—Invention No. 8, F major
Chopin—Trois Écossaises
Brahms—Hungarian Dance No. 1
Debussy—Prelude: Tierces Alternées

I have selected these at random, out of many hundreds equally good. They are of medium difficulty and exploit all kinds of tonal approaches that are best attained when the hands are free to fly above the keyboard.

Exaggerate hand motion as you practice. If you need visual help, mark arrows pointing downward at the beginning of each phrase and arrows pointing up at the end of each phrase. The "down" arrow should remind the student not just to press down the key with the finger but to use the weight of the arms to establish the timber. The "up" arrow means, "Throw your hands up, one foot above the keys." All staccatos except finger staccato and all rests require this movement during slow practice. If this becomes a habit, your music will not stay "in the piano"; your hands, your sounds, your musical concepts will be free, and your music will soar.

I realize that this is difficult for the beginner. The piano is a complex instrument, an orchestra within itself. Sitting in front of this massive piece of furniture, the neophyte is tempted to hang onto it to gain confidence, to lean on it, clutch at it, hit it with all his strength—and the piano, being a sensitive instrument, hits back; it exposes the young pianist's inexperience by sounding harsh, uneven, ragged, unpolished—just as the nervousness of a singer or string player is betrayed by uncontrolled vibrato. The student must learn that the piano is his friend and ally, his medium to express whatever he wants to say if he handles it properly.

CHAPTER FOUR

More about Practicing

Leopold Godowsky made a fine distinction between technique and mechanism: speed, fingerwork, octaves, according to him, fall into the latter category; they are separate problems, tools, while technique is all-conclusive. Technique implies complete mastery of the keyboard, including the ability to produce beautiful tone, to use the pedal sensitively, to memorize.

We must think of our piano as if it were part of us, or, rather, an extension of our equipment to express musical thought. Being a mechanical instrument, it is not the composer's medium; *that* honor is reserved for us who play. The audience must not even be conscious of the instrument; therefore, neither must we. We cannot play for an audience unless, or until, we have confidence in ourselves. In a way a concert artist is like a ski champion, who cannot expect to win unless he has complete command over the two pieces of wood attached to his feet; or like an actor who must completely submerge himself in his characterization to make it convincing. A musician cannot give a good performance unless he can forget about his instrument.

Technical mastery should not be considered an accomplishment in itself; it is the *sine qua non* of a virtuoso, the lowest rung of the ladder, the basic necessity, the starting point.

Chances are that three fourths of your repertoire will contain passages too difficult or awkward to be learned by practicing merely scales and arpeggios. We all have some little bête noire over which we stumble, and even though it may not throw us, it jars us and makes us expend so much thought and energy that we cannot concentrate properly on the rest of the composition.

Many technical exercise books have been written by Carl Czerny, Charles-Louis Hanon, Johann Pischna, a.o., for the purpose of training the fingers to overcome stumbling blocks in certain pieces. All this, however, solves only part of the problem. When you are through, you will know the exercises, but not the passage. The only solution is to make a special study of each little problem as it comes up, isolate it, turn it into an exercise, and after you have conquered the difficulty, put it back into the context of the composition.

Here is a list with subsequent illustrations:

Fingerwork cadenzas
Short technical passages
Staccato octaves, sixths
Chord jumps
Repeated notes
Ornamentation
Trills

Cadenza runs in rhythm framework
Syncopation
Fingering
Pedaling

In Chopin's Eb major Nocturne the final cadenza is a rapid cantilena passage; work on it all by itself, in rhythms and accents, and later with the metronome, starting slow and increasing in speed rate, as outlined in the previous chapter.

Illustration for "rhythm and accents":

(a) -... -... -... -... etc.
(b) .-.. .-.. .-.. .-.. etc.
(c) ..-. ..-. ..-. ..-. etc.
(d) ...- ...- ...- ...- etc.

This principle is applicable to any finger passage and can be adapted to any rhythm. For example, use a six-note group for the entire last movement of Beethoven's Sonata, Opus 32, No. 2, or a three-note group for Bach's D minor Prelude from the *Well-Tempered Clavier*, Book 1.

Or take such a handful as in Schubert's *Moment Musical* in F minor, ninth measure. Work at it very slowly, carefully pressing each key down to the very bottom; then transpose it and make a regular exercise of it (Illustration). Soon you will feel comfortable with the passage and won't have to think of it as a problem when you play the piece.

Another problem, in Schumann's *Papillons,* requires knowledge of keyboard reaction to hand bounce (Illustration). Mastering this, you will have acquired a skill that you can carry over to a great many similar problems, such as even the difficult octave passages in Liszt's *Hungarian Rhapsody No. 6.*

Illustrations of difficult passages made into finger exercises to solve specific problems: the first is from Measure 9 in Schubert's *Moment Musical* in F minor, the second from Measure 6 of the Polonaise, Section No. 11, in Schumann's *Papillons.* Such exercises should be practiced at metronome speeds from very slow gradually to correct tempo. The bounce your hands acquire in the Schumann can be used in various places; the same muscles are used when playing longer sustained passages of octaves and intervals such as the octave runs in the last movement of Beethoven's "Waldstein" Sonata, or the opening bars of the scherzo in Chopin's Bb minor Sonata.

When you play staccato octaves, such as those in the opening passage of Mendelssohn's G minor Concerto, make your hand into a stiff "octave mold," as I call it; the middle fingers curled under so that they will be out of the way (see end paper illustration). If you keep your hand in this position you will have clean, firm octaves, no matter where you put it down. In order to acquire this new habit, you might do octave scales in all the major and minor keys, slow to fast, with the metronome for a few days, until you get the feel of it. Then move this new skill back into the context of the concerto. This firm "mold" concept is useful for sixths, thirds, or any other interval used in rapid staccato passages such as the scales in sixths in the last movement of Saint-Saëns's G minor Concerto. When you have long octave passages that require endurance, such as the left-hand octave section in Chopin's Polonaise, Opus 53, and the right-hand passages in Liszt's Hungarian Rhapsody No. 6, you must work with the metronome very slowly and repeat the passage four times without stopping at each metronome speed from slow to fast, in order to build up the necessary power of endurance. You will suffer physical pain and learn to endure it; pain is like a tunnel of fire that forges muscles of steel. You will emerge at the other end after a long and trying period, invigorated, with a tremendous margin of reserve, and with the knowledge of complete mastery, which is well worth the effort.

A passage requiring accurate jumping of the hands from one part of the keyboard to another requires help from the eyes. Practice very slowly and use the metronome. Don't look at the center of the keyboard but at the keys you wish to strike at the extreme right or left.

Sometimes both hands have to jump simultaneously in opposite directions (such as the final chord bars of the bravura section from the scherzo of Chopin's Bb minor Sonata). Practice hands separately at first, then, when you put both hands together, look at the weaker one—at the left if you are right-handed, and at the right if you are left-handed. Take two of the jumping quarter notes and repeat back and forth until you can hit accurately ten times consecutively, then the next two, etc. If you continue to have trouble, use the "junior developer formula" (illustrated on P. 48) on this type of passage. This problem takes patience, time, and effort at the first learning, much less at each relearning.

When you come across a passage of repeated notes, as in Chopin's Grande Valse Brilliante No. 1, make an exercise of it. I always recommend changing fingers on repeated-note passages, because in this way you will rely on fingers rather than on piano action. Practice this exercise for a while on the closed keyboard lid by tapping the fingering out with correct accent on the wood to get the *feel* of the passage. When it sounds right here, it will be easier to make it sound right on the keys.

Exercise for repeated notes.

I learned to perform mordents, appoggiaturas, crossed appoggiaturas, trills and trill endings, turns, and all sorts of fussy ornamentation in this way: Play the desired mordent, trill ending, or whatever pattern is bothersome, four times in C major, four times in D flat major, four times in D major, etc., all the way up and down the chromatic scale. Learn to do mordents in all possible fingerings: 132, 232, 243, 343, 354, 454, and in both hands. You are teaching necessary patterns to the muscles.

In the same way, going up and down the chromatic scale, trills should be practiced with every possible finger combination: 13, 23, 24, 34, 35, 45; same procedure for the left hand. A slight loose-wrist motion is desirable. A four-finger trill combination (1323) is not recommended, because it puts too much responsibility on the fingers alone. Use the metronome slowly at first, perhaps only four notes at a beat of 80; always aim at steadiness rather than speed.

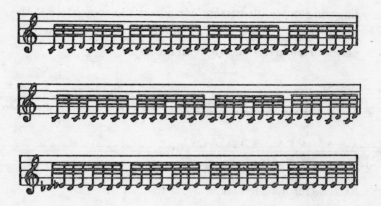

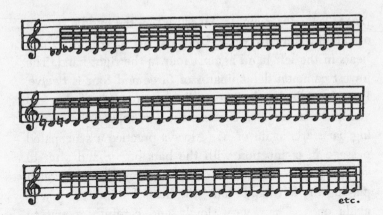

When there is a long cadenza in one hand while the other hand maintains the rhythm, I count the number of notes in the cadenza and divide the total by the number of beats it must fill. I practice with exaggerated accents on the notes where the beats should fall until I get the feel of the rhythm. Chopin's Prelude, Opus 28, No. 18, is a good example. Similarly, when the piano has a recitative against an orchestral accompaniment, such as in the second movements of Liszt's Concerto No. 1 and Chopin's Concerto No. 2, the soloist and conductor sometimes establish imaginary accents as anchors until they have performed the work together so many times that such anchors are no longer necessary.

Syncopation is another difficult problem with an easy, if painstaking, solution. Find the lowest common denominator of both rhythms and, working very slowly, count in terms of the denominator so that both rhythms fall into

MUSIC AT YOUR FINGERTIPS

place. Take, for example, Measure 8 in the middle section of Chopin's famous Valse, Opus 64, No. 1. We have three beats in the left hand against four in the right hand. The lowest common denominator of three and four is twelve. Play the right hand alone while you count to twelve and you find that the beat comes on 1, 4, 7, 10, and the following bar starts again on 1. (Always practice a syncopated passage in connection with the bars before and after to keep the syncopation in context.) Count to twelve again playing the left hand alone; the beats fall on 1, 5, 9, and again on 1. Then, very slowly and carefully, count to twelve while you play both hands together:

```
R H  —      —      —      —      —
     1  2  3  4  5  6  7  8  9  10  11  12/1
L H  —         —         —         —
```

Follow this diagram until you become accustomed to the *feel* of the two simultaneous rhythms. Then substitute a slow metronome beat for your verbal counting. Gradually increase the speed of the metronome. When you are sure that you feel it completely and the metronome is beating more than 150, divide the rate by three, the basic rhythm of the waltz; your metronome will now be at 50, and the beats should coincide with the left hand. It means a critical moment when you make this transition; be especially careful to proceed slowly and to keep everything in place. If necessary, go back to verbalizing the twelve counts until you are sure that you can rely on the metronome's three

44

beats. Then you can proceed to faster speeds up to the tempo of the composition. It will take time at first to absorb the feeling of syncopation, but you will be able to use the new skill always.

Fingering has made big strides since the days of Carl Philipp Emanuel Bach, who in his *True Art of Playing Keyboard Instruments* recommended for scales the fingering 1234512345, etc., instead of the conventional 121212! But it is impossible to give set fingering rules for any given passage, because what is good for a small hand may be awkward for a larger one. Personally, I recommend maintaining a similar fingering where a note pattern is repeated, so that the hands can keep a set routine. A good illustration is in Bach's C minor Prelude, of the *Well-Tempered Clavier*, Book 1, beginning with Measure 28. The right hand plays an eight-note pattern eight times, using the same fingering regardless of hand position: 32343231. In the same way the left hand repeats its pattern, using the same fingering regardless of hand position: 23212324. This principle eliminates the tendency to unconscious accents and is much simpler to memorize.

Wherever possible, use fingering to improve legato. Here is a legato fingering for what would otherwise be an extremely rough passage: Measure 2 of the *Un poco animato* section of the first movement of Saint-Saëns's Concerto No. 2 in G minor:

```
54 45 4543 4343 4535 4543 4343 2343 4534|5
32 12 1221 2121 2312 1221 2121 121  2312|3
```

Experiment with awkward passages and try every possibility. There is no law that says the thumb can't be used on black keys, or that the third and fourth fingers cannot follow the fifth in an ascending scale in the right hand or a descending scale in the left hand. For example, the last bars of Chopin's "Étude in Sixths" is easily negotiated by the conventional back-finger chromatic-scale fingering, with the thumb staccato on all the bottom notes. Often the thumb can be used as a pivot to keep a passage legato, as in the right hand of Chopin's Prelude, Opus 28, No. 23, or the left hand of Chopin's Prelude, Opus 28, No. 3.

In legato chord passages try to keep at least the melody line legato. Lean on it with your fingers, legato, while you pick up the other notes demi-marcato. Never depend on the pedal to do the work of the fingers. The second movement of Beethoven's "Pathétique" Sonata is a good illustration.

The pedal should be used only to enhance harmony and to help bind legato that the fingers can't manage. For best effect use it as little as possible. Never use the pedal when you can do without it. In pedaling, the ear is the only guide, since every piano reacts differently to it. In legato chord passages the pedal should be changed immediately *after* the chord is played. Practice this very slowly until the principle is understood. Chopin's Prelude No. 20, in C minor, is a good example. There are places in Debussy and in Busoni's arrangements of Bach's organ compositions where use of the sostenuto pedal is effective; but don't become too dependent on it, as some leading makes of European pianos don't have this tool. For people who are cultivating the *pp* to *p* dynamic range it is useful to practice Mozart and Haydn sonatas completely with soft pedal so that the ear is forced to work with a very low dynamic ceiling. This is not meant for performance, of course.

For really stubborn passages involving long finger work and octaves I use what I call "developers," because they build the passage in the hands and develop endurance at the same time. Here is the formula:

Take the first eight notes, accent the *ninth*, which is your pivot, after which you return to the beginning. Repeat four times. Then start on the *second* note, use the *tenth* note for a pivot, go back to the second, and repeat four times. Then start with the *third* note, etc., until the

Formula for "developers" using a C major scale as a model.

end of the passage. This can be used on the entire last movement of the B♭ minor Chopin Sonata; on the finger-work and octave passages in the last movement of the Tschaikovsky Concerto No. 1; on the octave work at the end of the Liszt Sonata.

For short but difficult passages I use a "junior" version of developers. Repeat the first two notes in sixteenths for four quarters. Proceed with the second and third notes for four quarters, proceed with the third and fourth notes, etc., to the end of the passage. Then start at the beginning,

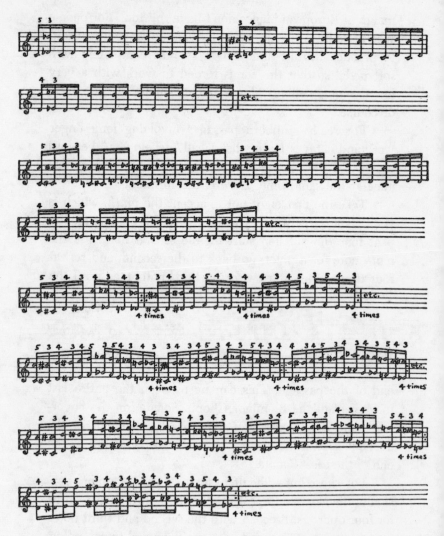

Formula for "junior developers" using a chromatic scale in octaves as a model.

play the first two notes, add the *third* as a pivot, return, repeat four times. Start with the *second* note, use the *fourth* as a pivot, repeat four times. Start with the *third* note, etc., to the end of the passage.

Next phase:

Start again with the first note of the passage and use the *fifth* note as a pivot.

Start again, and use the *seventh* note as a pivot.

The grouping of nine notes is the largest maneuverable for this kind of passage development. This can be used in such complicated passages as the tenth variation of Schumann's *Symphonic Études,* or the scale in fourths in the first movement of Chopin's B minor Sonata.

Dull, time-consuming work! But such daily practice over a period of time will almost guarantee absolute perfection at every performance. The possibility of becoming "derailed" is almost nil.

Don't exaggerate the fermata—it should hardly break the rhythmic pulse. Resist the temptation to take undue advantage of it.

I recommend playing all the repeats marked by the composer. In scherzi, architecture demands it; in sonatas, only impatience denies it. Music is not supposed to be a hurried affair, and if the composer thought a repeat necessary for the full absorption of his music, obey him! You are familiar with every note, but your listeners may be glad of a second chance to recognize sonata themes.

Try not to place undue emphasis on unimportant parts of the music. It can distract from really important material.

Interpretation

√ [Never play a phrase twice in exactly the same way. Examine the context in which the twin phrases appear, and use your imagination if there are no composer markings to establish their direction. Sometimes a softer imitation of the first phrase is appropriate. At other times both phrases are steps toward a greater climax. The composer meant to emphasize mood by repetition; define it.) Examples are Chopin's Ballade No. 4 and Haydn's Variations in F minor.

When you have a tremolo or repeated accompaniment figure, create an effect with the whole passage rather than awareness of individual notes. Examples are the left-hand octave tremolo in the first movement of Beethoven's "Pathétique" and the right-hand figuration in Rachmaninoff's Prelude in G♯ minor.

However, before assigning an accompaniment figure to the role of mood setter, be sure that it is not a melody in its own right. In the first movement of Beethoven's Sonata, Opus 14, No. 1, the arpeggio figures are so important melodically that use of pedal cannot be recommended because this would cloud their lyrical clarity.

Small hands often find it necessary to roll or break a chord. If you are in this position—as I am—you will have to find a way of doing it in a manner that will not impair the music. Remember that besides breaking a chord from left to right (bottom to top) it can be done the other way around if it agrees better with the context of the music. Better still, play as many solid notes as possible *on the beat*, the remaining notes *afterward,* so that the essential rhythm won't be disturbed. For example, in the opening chords of Rachmaninoff's Second Concerto, play the left thumb quietly after all the other notes have been struck simultaneously.

Both portamento and rounded phrase types of legato should be cultivated. Each has its place and sometimes the quality of a piano's touch will require you to interchange them. When I was studying Chopin's F minor Nocturne, Opus 55, No. 1, for the first time, Cortot recommended a portamento-type legato with the full weight of the wrist and hand resting separately on each tone, while Rachmaninoff recommended a rounded-phrase legato emanating from the fingertips and guided by the wrist and elbow like tracing a semicircle, so that the tone would float in one circular arc from the beginning to the very end of the phrase. Both methods produced good results, and only the pianist can decide which type legato to use. For instance, in Schumann's "Strange Lands and People," from *Scenes from Childhood,* the lyrical style definitely calls for the round-phrase legato, while in Schubert's Impromptu in A flat major the portamento type seems more appropriate.

Memory should be such an integral part of the absorbing process of learning a new composition that it happens spontaneously, without forcing. However, if you have to speed the memory process, you can work on the section to be memorized first thing in the morning when your mind is fresh, and review it thoroughly for a half hour at the end of each practice period, and always before bedtime. Sometimes, if the problem is particularly knotty, it is helpful to take the music to bed and review it mentally, playing and hearing the notes in your mind with occasional glances at the score. While you sleep, what you have been learning will settle in your subconscious.

Ear training is very important, and more people than we realize have absolute or relative pitch that can be developed. Only about two per cent of the population is biologically tone deaf. The trained listener has a decided advantage in learning music; every effort should be made to develop the inner and outer listening abilities. Nadia Boulanger had me do all my harmony lessons away from the piano in order to develop the capacities of my inner ear. At first we must train our consciousness of rhythm and melodic curve by singing the melody we are learning. Later, when we start to play polyphonic music, we can sing or hum one melody while we play the other. When we learn a concerto we can sing important cues, in places where the solo instrument has to accompany or blend in with the orchestra.

Practicing a concerto, the pianist must realize that, whatever the quality or size of the orchestra with which he plays—whether it is one of the great ensembles of the world, a student orchestra, or an amateur group—performing a concerto is a collaboration. You cannot play the work alone. You must earn the orchestra's respect for your musical concept and must make them want to work with you, not against you. It is rarely the orchestra's or the conductor's fault when the results are not to the pianist's satisfaction. Try to sing the orchestral fill-ins; this will help you to listen to the orchestra. Talk to the conductor about your concept and mark what he has to say; often you will learn things of great importance by this communication of thoughts. A good conductor is a most highly trained listener, sometimes better equipped to help you in your interpretation than teachers or colleagues. Before rehearsals start, discuss special problems with your conductor and you will both adjust and blend your thoughts to the benefit of the joint production. Let the conductor handle his men and don't interfere; they are his instrument as the piano is yours. But help him. Watch him.

Keeping our own abilities in their proper perspective with our concepts, as compared with other artists' abilities, is extremely important. "Thou shalt not covet thy neighbor's goods" is a commandment that seems especially appropriate for musicians. It is futile to covet someone else's physical assets, such as quick memorizing ability or large hands, and it is well within the realm of possibility to develop your own resources. It is said that the 'cellist Gregor Piatigorsky can learn a whole composition en route in an airplane or train, fixing everything in his mind without even touching his instrument, and play it perfectly on arrival. We who are not so gifted, who must learn the slow, hard, no-short-cut way, can rarely concentrate on more than one thing at a time, but we can work during worktime, play during playtime, and generally find a time and place for everything without living on our bravado, nerve, or accomplishing the seemingly miraculous. Having large hands is not the panacea that so many people think it to be; Rachmaninoff used to complain about his big hands, and Artur Schnabel said that his thick fingers often got in his way. No matter how unfortunate you think your physical pianistic defects are, you can always make the most of overcoming them.

Do not ape and imitate every idea in interpretation you like. Interpretational concepts are very personal; diamonds in one person's hands may be glass splinters in another's. In music mere imitation always sounds synthetic. Only the genuine individual idea, based on a careful study of a score and a composer's personality, is convincing.

Here are two stories that involve the same composition and two opposing viewpoints:

(a) When the pianist Soulima Stravinsky (Igor Stravinsky's son), was living in Paris as a student, he had the great desire to master Liszt's *Feux Follets*. He went to Vladimir Horowitz, who gave him practice suggestions that he followed over a period of time. Apparently still unable to master *Feux Follets*, he returned to Horowitz and was told: "It is within the province of some of us to accomplish certain things at the piano, while others among us just are never capable of mastering certain problems. Don't worry about it; you are a great pianist just the same."

(b) When I was about eleven, I asked Rachmaninoff what he considered the most technically difficult piece written for piano. He deliberated for a few minutes then said, "Well, I suppose that one of the most difficult compositions is the Liszt étude *Feux Follets*." "I want to play it." "Oh no, not with your small hands. You could not do it yet." Now I knew I *had* to master it. I set to work and made up crazy, 'unorthodox fingering, broke passages into two hands, used hand positions that would have made Leschetizky turn in his grave, but I played all the notes and eventually mastered *Feux Follets*.

The point I'm trying to make is that the pianistic problem doesn't exist that cannot be solved by determined imagination. No individual, no book, has all the answers. Many of the most important solutions are in *your* head, *your* heart, *your* hands.

CHAPTER FIVE

Absorption and Projection

A COMPOSITION isn't learned; it is absorbed. It becomes as much a part of you as a finger or a tooth; even better because, along with your mental faculties, it usually improves with age. But before you can absorb a new piece of music, you must be absorbed by it. Your attitude will not be too different from being in love: unconditional fascination, desire to understand weaknesses or roughnesses, willingness to give a great deal of yourself in order to receive. Mastery of a work of art must be earned. Never be overawed by technical difficulties. A composition may have been written by a musical genius, but even the greatest genius is, first and foremost, a human being, an imaginative human being who wants to share the fruit of his creative upheaval with petty mortals like you and me. It is ours for the taking, with his blessing.

In the preceding chapters I have discussed the problems of proper practicing that apply to the recitalist as well as to the beginner. Even the most accomplished of my colleagues did his first scales at some time in his childhood. As an old Chinese proverb says, even the longest journey starts with a single step.

The first step is to get acquainted with what I call the "musical geography" of a new composition; we have to decide how we want it to sound. Then, I repeat, we play it very slowly, making sure that all the notes and markings are there; we experiment with pedal and fingering, and repeat the easier themes in as accomplished a manner as possible to get them "into our fingers" and sense the general pulse of the melody within the context of the composition. We do this several times a day, meantime proceeding to the difficult passages, subjecting them to the same process. We continue to experiment with the fingering until it feels comfortable. For intricate fingerwork we use the device of accents and rhythms described in the preceding two chapters. We may find it necessary to practice both hands separately, using the metronome, then finally repeat the whole procedure with both hands together: "developers," rhythms and accents, daily metronome drill. When each difficult passage has been conquered in this manner, we can usually play all the way from beginning to end without stopping and without making mistakes. Even if the tempo is still slow, we are beginning to make music. We put lilt into our themes, we work on the phrasing of our lyrical sections, we begin to *feel* the composition even though we may not yet project it.

However, all these devices should not be used in fugues or polyphonic passages, since they require concentration on many voices simultaneously. I like to mark theme entrances in fugues with colored pencils, to make the eye, as well as the ear, alert to the musical architecture from the start. Artificial accents and rhythms as a learning device here are as impossible and confusing as the willful distortion of tone volume.

Actually, I give a daily run-through to every composition I have in the works. It helps me to memorize it, or, rather, not to forget it. A pianist must know his music so thoroughly by heart that he can write it down, accurate to the last detail, at a split second's notice. Daily run-throughs are enormous timesavers. Even before we master a composition, little sections will begin to memorize themselves as they become absorbed by our subconscious. First they are like little islands; then some measures before, some measures after, stick to the memory, and together with the transitions whole large sections begin to take shape. Soon, working on the whole composition from beginning to end, from slow to fast, day by day, I gradually find myself turning fewer and fewer pages. Eventually the little islands merge into the whole large entity of the piece, which becomes mine entirely.

At that stage a piece appears to me like a newly born puppy—miraculous and exciting—because, though it quite clearly shows how it will look in the future, it still is clumsy in its spindly, young, inexperienced state. Carefully practicing every day, the pianist can concentrate on becoming more pliable, more sensitive to interpretational ideas; he can start to experiment with performance. Until now all his mental and physical faculties were tied closely with taking in; now he has to aim at that state of satiation and abundance where he can give.

Put down the music rack and open your piano all the way. You are going to project for the first time. You never heard this composition in quite that way before, and all sorts of new discoveries in the music and in your reaction to it lie ahead. Now, by opening the piano, you are changing one of the listening habits you have formed in practice.

Soon other small habits will change, purely physical habits: I put telephone books on my chair to give myself a different position; then, again, I play the same piece sitting on a low kitchen stool. I have to do something similar all the time on tour. Every pianist has a favorite height for his tabouret, and practically all piano benches are adjustable, but sometimes the exertion of playing a particular piano requires a different body position. Also, the change of seating height helps me to "loosen up," to get a free, unhampered feeling. Singers and violinists who are not glued to their instruments have different methods to get this feeling of physical freedom. Feodor Chaliapin was an impressive, dynamic, giant figure as he strode across his living room in the Hotel Ansonia, intoning some Russian folk melody. The singers Rosa Ponselle and Elizabeth Rethberg used to walk around their small dressing rooms at the Met, vocalizing before a performance. Violinists Nathan Milstein and Mischa Elman walk up and down as they warm up their fingers. A feeling of space and freedom is imperative for projection.

I occasionally play a new piece unexpectedly, on the spur of the moment, at odd times not on my practice schedule. Each time I listen critically and try to profit from every mistake. Am I making the music say what I intend? I ask an indulgent friend or relative to be my first audience. Then I take the composition out of my home environment;

I try it out at a piano store, at a friend's house. This is, in a way, as if my performance would have to earn its wings by experimental flight.

There is the story of a rich old gentleman who decided to take piano lessons, bought a concert grand, and practiced faithfully every day, despite the amusement of his friends and their warning that "you can't teach an old dog new tricks." Once a week the movers would come, take the piano away, and bring it back several hours later. The old gentleman's explanation: "I took it along to my piano lesson." This story is supposed to be funny, but to me it isn't; many pianists depend on their own instruments and are completely lost when they have to use a different one. Independence from outside factors is a performer's stock in trade.

Here are a few important things to watch out for, particularly for the student:

(1) Don't get discouraged during any part of the learning process. "The darkest hour is that before the dawn." Sometimes it may seem to you that for days, perhaps months, you cannot get anywhere with a certain composition, yet you will master it eventually. You may have to give it a rest for a few days. You may have become too closely involved with the composition for clear self-criticism; you may have "overpracticed," grown tense. The chances are that you will be amazed at how well it goes after a brief interval, but if it doesn't, you were not ready and you'd have had to start all over anyway. Just don't give up!

(2) Always have your music handy when you practice so that you can refer to it whenever you have the slightest question. Also, use the most authentic edition you can find and be sure to obey all the markings; thus you will never have to doubt the authority of your performance. If someone offers a suggestion, listen with an open mind, but consult the score before you follow it. (This is not required for fingering and pedaling, however, which are rarely written in by the composer himself; only remember that strong fingers are better than a heavy foot.) Never choose "tradition" over the indications in the original score. Tradition is a much-abused word; Toscanini defined it as "the last bad performance." To his last recording session the maestro studied and restudied the scores he had conducted for decades and the slightest doubt would send him back to the libraries hunting for the original manuscript. Tradition, for him, could be established only by the composer. Never take accepted practice for granted. When a child I played a Beethoven sonata for Wilhelm Backhaus, and he corrected a passage in it, but at home I rejected his correction and practiced it the way I wanted. The next time I played it for him he stopped me. "Mr. Backhaus," I said, "I see it differently. Why must I play it your way?" His simple reply I shall always remember: "Because that's how Beethoven wrote it."

(3) Be careful not to overaccent, or to place an accent where none was written. Most students go through such a stage and it is perfectly normal while learning a composition. The accents are like road marks that you need badly

on strange territory. Once you are more familiar with a road, you may still want to have the map handy, but you no longer have to slow down to read what the road sign says. After you have traveled the road frequently and come to know it well, you won't even notice the markers and will enjoy the scenery. As you play, watch out for your little accents and exaggerations, and eliminate them. They won't help you in performance and may damage your interpretation.

(4) Don't exaggerate your teacher's suggestion. When I first played a Chopin waltz for Alfred Cortot, he found my bass notes on the first beat too soft and lacking in rhythmic character. "Your basses have no substance; they don't support the melody. Make your first beats in the left hand at least as firm as this match," he said, and lit a cigarette. At home I tried to make my left hand first beats, not only in this piece but in everything else I played, as firm as, not a match, but a piano leg. This went on until it was explained to me that (a) exaggeration could lead to distortion and (b) we must not use the same device for different compositions unless it is in character. For example, a Viennese waltz by Strauss will gain by the now traditional lilting hesitation between the second and third beat, but a Chopin waltz would be ruined if played in that manner.

(5) Avoid mannerisms. Theatricals went out of fashion with the silent movies, in which gestures had to tell the whole story without the spoken word. At the piano

mannerisms are not only in bad taste but physically im-possible except for artists who are not really engrossed in the music. Besides, the natural, effortless abandon that comes with good, relaxed piano technique is sufficiently spectacular in itself.

CHAPTER SIX

Acquiring a Repertoire

PIANO REPERTOIRE is vast. Most great composers were pianists, choosing the piano rather than a string instrument because the polyphonic nature of the keyboard gives a more satisfying outlet for artistic self-expression. In the old days, before the great masters had composed our repertoires, they had to write their own music when they performed or taught. Bach wrote most of his many inventions for his many children; Mozart, Beethoven, Chopin, Schumann, Liszt wrote music for themselves or for their students. They wrote it, of course, in a way to make the best of the shape of their hands, their special abilities, their favorite devices. Composing his rhapsodies and operatic paraphrases, Liszt was playing to the public in much the same way as our band leaders do today when they arrange hit songs for their ensembles. He took full advantage of his large hands by writing octave and arpeggio passages, such as in his arrangements of Paganini's études, which were so difficult that, for many years, no other pianist could play them. Delicate Chopin, on the other hand, gave preference to the type of composition that sounds best in a salon.

In a similar manner the amateur pianist will choose a repertoire that will emphasize his best qualities; yet knowledge of piano literature should be well rounded, and a good teacher will always try to arouse a student's curiosity and guide his taste toward a comprehensive repertoire. To fit one's repertoire to one's personality does not mean to take the line of least resistance.

Some professional musicians keep repertoire books in which they list all the compositions they have ever performed, together with dates, places, exact timings, and, if a partner or an orchestra was involved, comments about rehearsals. A professional can't remember everything he has ever studied. The book will remind him of musical experiences and triumphs half forgotten. It is like an inventory; a quick glance will indicate where the repertoire is strong and where it needs to be built up. For the student it is also an excellent progress log, and it is a real morale booster when the going gets tough to see, in black and white, the amount of music already mastered.

Our present tendency toward specialization has also slipped into the concert hall: some artists prefer to play Chopin and other romantics, others specialize in Bach and the early classics, others in Beethoven and Brahms, and there are even some who play mostly contemporary music. I don't think this is good unless a musician's actual repertoire is well balanced and he is able to perform a healthy cross-section of piano literature. Paderewski had a very small repertoire, but it was comprehensive and large enough to make several interesting programs.

When an artist has a well-balanced program, his special fields will stand out in much better perspective. I tell my students to think of general repertoire as the main trunk of a tree; they can explore one branch or another with all its twigs and leaves, but then they should return to the trunk and add what they have learned to strengthen the whole miraculous structure. Later they can explore a different branch, and use the newly acquired knowledge to make the main trunk stronger still. Walter Gieseking, who was famous for his playing of Bach, Mozart, Beethoven, Schumann, and in particular Debussy and Ravel, learned what was for him a completely new musical color, Rachmaninoff's Piano Concerto No. 2, toward the end of his career, and played it for the first time at the Hollywood Bowl when he was over sixty. Toscanini seldom conducted Tschaikowsky until Horowitz became his son-in-law and persuaded him to accompany him in the Piano Concerto No. 1. The record they made is among the most outstanding, and the maestro was then almost seventy years old.

The two things I caution my students against are arrangements from other instruments, and simplifications of music they cannot play in the original. I also recommend the utmost caution in the choice of sets of variations for a concert program; variations are tiresome for the average listener unless they are short and written by one of the great masters.

Repertoire building begins at an early age; therefore, the same principles apply to both the amateur and the professional. When it begins—or ought to begin—there will be one youngster in a million who will become a child prodigy, and one in a hundred thousand who can be expected, with a fair amount of certainty, to have a musical career. In repertoire building the point of departure is the same for the budding Myra Hess as for the home-town girl, whose only audience will be the captive one of family and neighbors.

✓ Very young children of preschool age absorb a foreign language more easily than later, and this also applies to the language of music. Small children can perform marvels of retention quite beyond the comprehension of adults. When I was four, I memorized a Bach invention in half an hour, just before a matinee, and played it as an encore. I would never dream of doing such a thing today.

Some youngsters in their preteens can learn a sonata in a week, a concerto in two weeks. Later it takes longer to assimilate, because then we become aware of many other elements to be absorbed along with the notes. This may be the reason why so many artists with large repertoires were child prodigies who started to accumulate reppertoire when they were very young. When Leopold Godowsky, who was known for his tremendous repertoire, was in his forties, composing, teaching, touring, someone asked him how he found time to learn new things. He replied, "I don't learn them, I know them."

Since the compositions we remember longest are those we have learned during our formative years, the teacher has a particular responsibility toward the student who wants to become a professional to be sure that each piece of music he learns can become part of a permanent backlog. For example, a talented pupil will have more oppor-

67

tunity to play Beethoven's Sonata, Opus 27, No. 1, than the "Moonlight," Opus 27, No. 2. It will teach him the same things technically, but if he plays it later in public it will be unhackneyed. It is better for a young musician not to provoke comparisons with the Serkins and Rubinsteins, but to be noted for courage and personality. For the same reason I find it hard to understand why most pedagogues assign Chopin's Ballade No. 1, Scherzo No. 2, Fantasie-Impromptu, the C# minor Valse, and the like, when similar, but less familiar works, such as the Ballade No. 2, Scherzo No. 4, Impromptu No. 3, and the F minor Valse would be better investments in terms of learning time. The pianist will have to learn the better-known repertoire later on anyway, and he will be able to do so by himself.

There is a definite place for the better-known repertoire in the teacher's studio: with the less talented pupil who is sure that he will never play in public and who studies for the sake of making music rather than for the intangible dream of becoming the world's most famous recitalist. To the teacher whose pupils want to play popular music I say, "Why not?" Use it as reading material to give them the thrill they seek in playing the music in vogue with their set of young friends, teaching them a valuable skill at the same time. The student who cannot absorb much of harmony or Bach might still play well enough, and should be encouraged along the lines of short melodious works by Grieg, Mendelssohn, Schumann, Chopin, Mozart, Haydn, Bartók. Many teachers give their students very good starts with the Edwin Hughes Master Series books of unadulterated but easier selections from the great composers.

The teacher should always be on the lookout for good intermediate material that has not been simplified and revised by editors. New collections in all fields of music, including contemporary, are being released on the market constantly, and the teacher should keep posted on all this good learning literature.

The ideal repertoire-building system for most students seems to be to learn three compositions from different musical periods and of varied styles simultaneously. For instance the youngster who is practicing a Bach gavotte, a Chopin prelude, and Prokofieff's *Fairy Tale* at the same time enjoys such a pleasant variety of musical fare that he cannot become bored with any aspect of his practicing. The same principle of three contrasting irons in the fire can be maintained at all levels of instruction.

The teacher should have a long-range-potential repertoire plan for each pupil, the details of which can be flexible according to the student's progress. For instance, there is the problem of the student whose present piano ability is flashy but sloppy and who feels that he must play, say, Grieg's Piano Concerto. Now, the pupil probably could be pushed, even though most of the passages are beyond him. By trying hard and with great patience on the parts of teacher, pupil, and the pupil's family who have to hear him practice, he may play at the end of one year the first movement through from beginning to end with a lot of wrong notes. It is better to aim toward the Grieg Concerto gradually by mastering a few of Grieg's *Lyrical Pieces*, a couple of Mendelssohn's *Songs without Words*, a Schubert impromptu, a couple of Chopin's preludes and a mazurka, a Scarlatti sonata, a Mozart fantasy, a Kabalevsky sonatina, and finally, at the end of two years, Grieg's entire Piano Concerto, which could have been "softened up" all along in the student's spare time. It will come easily and sound well because the student has prepared for it properly and has learned a lot on how to practice—to say nothing of other first-class pleasurable music into the bargain!

It is important to advance a student according to his intellectual and pianistic capacity. For the young student whose hands can't yet span octaves there is plenty of attractive music that doesn't require octaves; such compositions are far superior to cut-down versions of the more difficult work that will sound weak in the undeveloped hands and will spell discouragement to the immature mind that does not understand why the piece doesn't "sound right." A pianist with a naturally beautiful tone, but as yet undeveloped power, can play wonderful repertoire, ranging from Frescobaldi and Purcell to Handel, that is completely overlooked by people who delight in exhibiting a powerful technique. A pupil who has good fingers, but whose intellectual power is still potential, can play Weber, Tschaikowsky, Hummel, etc.

The ability to learn is something that grows within a person as long as he keeps this ability active. What a great inspiration is someone like Mischa Elman, who, after fifty glorious years on the stage, still has the youthful musical stamina and vigor to learn new music! Artur Rubinstein, despite his statement that he had no formal lessons after the age of fourteen, learned the most important lesson of all—how to think for himself and let experience be his teacher. Rachmaninoff felt that as long as one practiced the hands would remain supple, and continuing to learn keeps the mind young.

Teachers often mourn the loss of a good pupil. This is so unnecessary. Nadia Boulanger described the teaching process as a game of give-and-take. Arnold Schoenberg starts the preface to his *Harmonienlehre* with the words, "My pupils taught me this book," meaning their questions and their mistakes. Teacher and pupil inspire each other with fresh ideas, but they may reach a period of diminishing returns. At this time both gain from seeking fresh fields to grow within themselves and to enrich others. The really great teachers, such as Franz Liszt and Ferruccio Busoni, never had pupils in the ordinary sense of the word, but disciples and friends who discussed, played for each other, and grew together.

The real musician will be forever seeking new means of projection, looking over new literature, making up experimental programs. Art has no boundaries and the horizons of accomplishments are always beckoning with new challenges.

CHAPTER SEVEN

Building a Concert Program

PROGRAM BUILDING is a difficult art and should never be attempted hastily or casually. There are different kinds of programs, each with its own intrinsic laws.

A full recital, meaning a variety concert program, should present examples of the various composers' finest music. It will naturally show the performer at his best. It should be a healthy mixture of familiar and less familiar music, including at least one modern composer to convey the feeling that music is a contemporary, living thing.

Short group programs have an entirely different basis. Here the pianist has no more than fifteen minutes to show his ability to best advantage. To me the best formula is to use a bright opening number, then a contrasting slow work (but not too slow in order not to break the momentum of the group), and a brilliant finale demonstrating technical prowess. Have a bright encore ready. And play only whole compositions; excerpts or single movements from sonatas or suites have no place on the programs of a serious artist.

There is also the "monochromatic" program, the

one-composer program, all-Beethoven, all-Chopin, all-Schumann, for example. The performer has to be careful to present a varied picture, a good, bird's-eye view of the composer's works: some of the strongest and most famous, some lesser-known ones, and others that illustrate particular characteristics and subtleties. In other words, it should be a well-rounded, comprehensive musical portrait of the man.

For a time "novelty programs" were in vogue. They consisted only of toccatas, or études, or preludes, etc., and had a certain educational value: they illustrated how different composers treated the same type of composition.

Like every fashion, that of program building is in a constant state of flux. Every ten years we have different heroes, villains, and whipping boys. One season there will be a "run" on Schumann's *Carnaval,* or the Liszt sonata, or Beethoven's "Appassionata," and for some seasons thereafter these works will take an enforced vacation, only to be revived again by a number of performers simultaneously.

For the person who is interested in the historical development of concert programs, the big libraries have fascinating material on the nature of successful programs in, say, the days of the Bach family. In the good old times a concert was a big social event, the talk of the town until the next concert. It often lasted for many hours, well into dawn, and included excerpts from solo sonatas, chamber music, symphonies, arias sung by leading singers; assisting artists often borrowed from variety shows—acrobats, magicians, jugglers. Beethoven once conducted a concert in which, between movements of one of his major works, a "violinist" demonstrated that he could play with his instrument held upside down. Improvisation on the piano was a major item; Mozart, Beethoven, Liszt were famous for their improvising even before they reached similar fame as composers. Often the theme would be a popular tune or current hit chosen by the audience. Otherwise almost everything was played from the score until the virtuoso days of Thalberg and Liszt, who revolutionized recital practice. When Clara Schumann, as a prodigy of twelve, returned to Germany from a tour and played by heart after the example of these two men, whom she had heard in Paris, she was severely criticized for her "unmusical desire to attract attention by circus tricks."

At the same time Liszt presented the first all-piano concerts and, showman that he was, he sat so that the audience could see his handsome profile; formerly they always saw the performer's back. I firmly believe that only by learning about the past can we see the present in its proper perspective and dare participate in future developments. Liszt rightly said that Father Time was the most authentic music critic.

Wherever we live, whether in a hamlet or a metropolis, we are influenced by the cultural climate of the area. It is human nature to believe that local newspapers write the worthiest and most important opinions, that the local orchestra and its conductor occupy the most respected positions in the musical world, that our local music teachers dominate the area's musical thinking. When we travel and visit a larger city, perhaps another continent, we begin to get a truer picture. Since it is hard for most people to travel much, perhaps the best proxy method of keeping *au courant* with cultural events and styles is to subscribe to the most important paper of a musical metropolis, and keep a scrapbook of programs and reviews to follow the development of young talent; to watch, over a period of time, the trends in program making as they are molded by critics and public opinion. Why not make a hobby of studying young artists, their programs and reviews, their training background, their potential, and of trying to predict who will be the immortal of tomorrow? The history of the world is documented by cultural trends; it is fascinating to watch the relationship between world news and cultural achievements.

Working with the artist and repertoire producers at my recording company has taught me an important lesson in programming: that there need be no hard-and-fast rule of order in the list of compositions on a record. The same is true for a recital. For a quarter of a century we used to place music chronologically; to start with Scarlatti or Bach, proceed through the romantic period, delve into a modern or contemporary group, and end with a grand finale, usually a tried-and-true war horse, to bring down the house. Thousands of successful programs have been built along these lines. In fact it may be the adherence to this format that brings about the statement, every once in a while, that this generation will hear the last piano recital. So much good music is available on records and radio that audiences don't have to leave their comfortable living rooms unless enticed by an extraordinary event. But I still believe that an interesting program, carefully and tastefully built for variety, color, substance, and novelty, can get the most tired businessman out of his armchair and into the concert hall.

Ideally, your program should last about seventy minutes. Your first number should not be too long, so that the incorrigible late-comers don't have to feel that they are not getting their money's worth. I like a good and strong start because it puts the audience into an expectant frame of mind; also it should not display your full case of fireworks so that the mood of your program can crescendo with excitement. First choose your *pièce de résistance* and build around it: a masterwork like a sonata by Beethoven, Schumann, or Mozart; a Debussy suite; a Bach partita; any major work from any musical period. If you want to use two masterworks, choose contrasting ones from different musical periods and of different architecture—not two sonatas, two suites, etc., but preferably a sonata and a suite, or a set of variations. Also, if you have a very tuneful work, don't follow with another just as tuneful; your audience won't remember either melody; neither have two similar rhythms follow each other, such as two waltzes, or a waltz and a mazurka. To play a dramatic work just before intermission is excellent policy; as in the theater, it will create suspense. Then, after the intermission, you may play one of your long selections; people are rested and ready to give you their close attention. Don't have two compositions of the same genre unless you deliberately want to point up contrasting styles. To illustrate, don't

use a waltz by Schubert and a waltz by Chopin, but do use
a prelude and fugue by Bach and a prelude and fugue
by Shostakovitch. Sometimes it is very effective to have
two contrasting compositions in the same key or relative
key—a nocturne and an étude perhaps—succeed each
other; this is like placing a light blue flower next to a
dark blue, one enhancing the other's shade. When you
have several short compositions, don't program them in
a monotonous row, such as slow-fast-slow-fast; better use
a variety of musical shades, such as soft and sad, quick
fingers, melodious and dramatic, brilliant fireworks. Get
as many different moods into your programs as possible.
Place your soft, slow pieces to best advantage when the
public needs a rest from something dramatic. Don't let
your program lag on the penultimate number; use a fast
nocturne or a slow waltz, or a catchy light melody; your
program must keep its sweeping momentum. Let your encores be a continuation of your program in quality and in
added colors. If you have a favorite composition that you,
in a way, identify with personal experience, make it your
last encore always, like a signature at the bottom of a
painting.

Audiences in different parts of the world require
different programs. Germans have a long musical tradition
and like a heavier program of pure music with at least
two major works that will challenge their intellect. The
Gallic and Latin audiences prefer to be entertained with
a majority of lighter compositions. The English, Dutch,
and Scandinavians are slow to express their reactions, but

they are extremely alert and intelligent listeners who require a carefully balanced program of abstract and contemporary works. In general, European audiences are very sophisticated. The Brazilians and Argentines have made a national hero of Chopin. For South Americans concerts by internationally known artists are major events and they have exacting ideas of performance, shaped by constant listening to recordings of the world's greatest. They expect performers to have an individual, identifiable style; more than anywhere else, performers are judged on the basis of pure ability, plus the way in which they play Chopin.

Frequently professionals judge the quality of young debut artists by the originality and care that go into the building of their programs. Even for an experienced performer it takes a long time—sometimes weeks of concentrated thought, effort, and research—to assemble a topnotch variety program on which they will stake their reputation for a concert season.

Let us now analyze several representative concert programs:

PROGRAM BY VLADIMIR HOROWITZ

Sonata in Eb major	Haydn
Two Songs without Words:	Mendelssohn
May Time	
Shepherd's Complaint	
Pictures at an Exhibition	Moussorgsky

Impromptu in A♭ major	Chopin
Nocturne in F♯ major	Chopin
Ballade in G minor	Chopin
Serenade to a Doll	Debussy
Étude for Four Fingers	Debussy
Toccata, Opus 11	Prokofieff

Analysis

The central feature is Moussorgsky's *Pictures*. Notice the variety in mood from the beginning to the end of the program; never once is a color repeated.

The Haydn is a classic, pristine, yet bright opening number. The two contrasting Mendelssohn songs whet the listeners' appetite for the monumental romantic Moussorgsky suite.

The intermission gives the public a rest, and the familiar Chopin compositions afterward will not tax their stamina. The two contrasting Debussy pieces are both a balance for the two Mendelssohn songs heard earlier and a relief between the lyricism of Chopin and the steely brilliance of Prokofieff.

Possible criticism

The main work, *Pictures,* was not the original composition but his own arrangement; there is so much fine piano music available that arrangements can easily be avoided.

Program by Artur Rubinstein

Chaconne	Bach-Busoni
Sonata in E♭, Opus 81a ("Les Adieux")	Beethoven
Intermezzo in B♭ minor, Opus 117, No. 2	Brahms
Capriccio in B minor, Opus 76, No. 2	Brahms
Rhapsody inE♭ major, Opus 119, No. 4	Brahms

INTERMISSION

Polka, "The Golden Age"	Shostakovich
Vision Fugitive, Opus 22	Prokofieff
Suggestion Diabolique, Opus 4, No. 4	Prokofieff
Barcarolle, Opus 60	Chopin
Nocturne in C♯ minor, Opus 27, No. 1	Chopin
Polonaise in A♭ major, Opus 61	Chopin

Analysis

For color, variety of rhythm, pace, mood this program is exemplary. Rubinstein, knowing how chary of contemporary music an audience can be, wisely placed Shostakovich and Prokofieff before the Chopin group, which he uses as a great crescendo and climax. Notice his use of unhackneyed Chopin.

Possible criticism

This program is too full of sure-fire, smaller, familiar "desserts." It might be improved by playing the entire cycle of Brahms Opus 119, which ends with the Rhapsody, instead of using the Intermezzo and Capriccio from different groups. The cycle is a complete suite with the same continuity as a sonata, and it would add weight to the program without making it longer. It also would improve the balance, for there are only short pieces after intermission.

Shostakovich and Prokofieff are very similar in character; it would be better to contrast styles, using, for instance, Bartók, Poulenc, or Barber instead of Shostakovich.

The idea of using a Bach transcription is open to criticism among purists who argue that, inasmuch as Bach wrote so much keyboard music, it is not necessary to play a transcription from the violin.

PROGRAM BY DAME MYRA HESS

Rondo in D major, K. 485	Mozart
Adagio in B minor, K. 540	Mozart
Little Gigue in G major, K. 574	Mozart
Sonata in A major, Opus 120	Schubert

INTERMISSION

Partita No. 1	Bach
Sonata in C minor, Opus 111	Beethoven

Analysis

Here is an artist who uses the classics with imagination in building an interesting and charmingly songful program. The Mozart Adagio and Gigue and the A major Schubert sonata are seldom heard and have the effect of important rediscoveries in the hands of a master.

Notice the beautiful program balance: three short light classics before the romantic long Schubert, then, after intermission, the more familiar dance movements of Bach's classic Partita, leading to the last Beethoven sonata, a dramatic crescendo of magnificent music.

PROGRAM BY WALTER GIESEKING

Partita in B♭ major	Bach
Three Sonatas	Scarlatti
Fantasie in C major, Opus 17	Schumann

INTERMISSION

Barcarolle, Opus 60	Chopin
Pagodas	Debussy
Reflets dans l'Eau	Debussy
Rhapsody No. 9	Liszt

Analysis

This unusual program is admirably balanced. The artist wisely builds toward the focal composition, Schumann's Fantasie, to draw attention to the new romantic colors. He builds a crescendo up to intermission and then starts a decrescendo with Chopin, to reach the quietest possible mood with *Reflets*. Finally, the stunning Liszt

Rhapsody pulls the audience to their feet in a roaring climax.

At the same time Gieseking gives similar balance to each program half by including the short sonatas by Scarlatti, which represent different intensities of the same classic shading, to counterbalance the short pieces by Debussy, whose impressionistic, ethereal piano sound is his specialty.

ALL-SCHUMANN PROGRAM BY JOSEF LHÉVINNE

Études Symphoniques, Opus 13
Toccata, Opus 17
Four Pieces from *Fantasiestuecke,* Opus 12

INTERMISSION

Carnaval, Opus 9

Analysis

This is a magnificent, timeless program, which includes the two most famous works of Schumann, the *Études,* and *Carnaval.* Only captiousness would insist that one of the lesser-known sonatas should be substituted for one of these major works. The artist's interpretation of the hair-raising Toccata was one of the technical feats that made him famous; the introspective *Fantasiestuecke* makes the Schumann color palette complete. Notice the perfect balance in placing a long major work at the beginning, and another one after the intermission, when listeners usually are at their most receptive.

Caprice on the Departure of a Beloved Brother	Bach
Sonata in B♭, Opus 106 ("Hammerklavier")	Beethoven

INTERMISSION

12 Études, Opus 25	Chopin

Analysis

This program cannot fail. It is centered around the titanic "Hammerklavier" sonata, a work so difficult to carry off well that only half a dozen pianists per generation succeed. The Bach is a light, charming curtain raiser. After intermission comes a big surprise for Serkin fans: the second book of Chopin études is a major pianistic feat, outside the territory of this artist who specializes in the German-Austrian school.

Possible criticism

A short lyrical piece of more recent music, perhaps Prokofieff, Bartók, or Ginastera, between intermission and Chopin, would supply additional color.

PROGRAM BY RUTH SLENCZYNSKA

Sonata in D major, Opus 10, No. 3	Beethoven
Excursions	Barber
Ballade No. 2, in F major	Chopin
Étude, Opus 10, No. 1	Chopin

INTERMISSION

Carnaval	Schumann
Italian Polka	Rachmaninoff
Hungarian Rhapsody No. 15	Liszt

Analysis

This program was built around two contrasting works: an early classic, the Beethoven sonata, and the romantic *Carnaval*.

The juxtaposition of the sonata and the contemporary, almost jazzy American suite forms an interesting background for the two Chopin works.

The spectacular étude, with its broad sweep, placed before the intermission, uplifts the audience who will have to concentrate on the long *Carnaval*.

Rachmaninoff's unfamiliar Italian Polka is light, short, and tunefully dainty between the long, rich *Carnaval* and the fervent brilliance of Liszt's rhapsody.

Possible criticism

The four-movement Beethoven sonata is quite long

for an opening number. If a shorter sonata had been chosen, there might have been room for a complete, short, softly lyrical composition to round out better the variety of the program; the best place for such a melodic work would have been just before or just after the *Carnaval*.

But nothing could have been added to the program as it stood, which was brilliant, with good momentum.

CHAPTER EIGHT

Preparing a Program

PREPARING a program has very much the same aspects as preparing a fine meal. There is a deadline; there is a variety of different tasks to perform, and they all have to be at their peak at the same time.

For my personal schedule I advance the deadline by about six weeks, if possible. (Artists who travel almost all year round have to prepare much of their program en route; it is difficult, but it can be done.) A six-week margin usually leaves me some time to rest and to polish my program so that I am completely ready when concert time arrives.

It is possible to establish some sort of work schedule if you know approximately how much time you can give yourself every day. Four hours, preferably divided into two periods of two hours each, are a bare minimum. Each person's working capacity has a different rhythm, closely related to our physical condition, basic metabolism, body temperature. I see no point in fighting against it if you don't have to; you'll need your self-discipline for other aspects of your work. I'd rather suggest that you organize

87

your work accordingly and rotate your material so that you get the maximum return out of the time invested. Many people are at their best after breakfast and at their worst after lunch, and they wake up again when everybody else wants to go to dinner, which is very inconvenient but cannot be helped. I am a "night person" and my best times are early morning and late at night; my ideal daily practice schedule is three periods of two and a half hours each.

I warm up slowly; it takes me at least an hour of practice before I hit my learning stride. It is a difficult job—and I sometimes wonder whether any of us really likes to work—but the challenge is fascinating. Before a concert we all bemoan our miserable lives; afterward we wouldn't trade places with anyone else in the world.

No one is at his peak all the time. On some days our minds will be more alert; on others our best practice will be at the functional muscular level; a third time our interpretative powers seem to have special inspiration. When we rotate our practice material, we can take special advantage of these bright periods. Much of the time, dull days are a symptom of our reluctance to getting started. With a variety of different material on which to work we are sure to be fascinated by some aspect of the practice routine if we give it half a chance. Sigmund Freud said that laziness is simply fear of not succeeding; I have found that consistency of effort at least prevents total failure, even if the spark of inspiration eludes us temporarily.

Once we have definitely selected our program, we should start with the most difficult parts of it and begin to soften them up. I take the most intricate single composition to be learned and play it every day from beginning to end. I do this first thing during the morning period and spend at least one hour working it over to become closely familiar with it. Sometimes I spend the whole morning practicing this difficult new piece without even noticing the passing of time. This is good. I reserve at least half an hour, possibly an hour, of my evening practice, just before I stop for the day, for reviewing and smoothing down the same work.

If I am very tired after the morning's first hour, I start practicing on the most routine technical thing on the program. This gives my learning apparatus a rest while I exercise my fingers on material I will need. Metronome slow-to-fast practice is particularly good here because the forced steadiness has a calming effect and you have the comfort of resting mentally and accomplishing something at the same time.

Next, I suggest listing all the routine passages and starting with the most difficult one. As the days go by, the "most difficult" will come under control and you can be satisfied just to review it and proceed to the next problem, and so on down the line. The first hour of afternoon practice can be spent softening up the next-to-most-difficult new composition; the remainder of the afternoon session should repeat the morning's metronome practice. In the evening, depending on how tired you are, either start by softening up New Work No. 2 or repeat metronome practice for the third time. Always end a working day by a strong review of the most difficult new work.

This is Phase No. 1, the "ugly duckling" stage we all go through when we haven't a thing ready to play except maintenance repertoire we have in hand without special practice. It is good for an emergency, but not gratifying to play when preoccupied with new and exciting material.

As we put most of our time into Composition No. 1, learning it as described before, part of it will eventually reach the finished stage. We put the finished parts aside for the time being and concentrate on the stubborn section. When we have conquered these, we forget the whole work for a while and promote ourselves to No. 2. We finish this and replace it by No. 3, etc. As we proceed we eventually find that we have covered the whole program and whatever encores we have in mind—three are the ideal number.

Now comes Phase No. 2: divide the whole program and encores into three parts from beginning to end. If you have three practice periods, spend the first two hours of each on playing through one program part at a time, just as if you were playing the concert. Get into the spirit of each phrase of every note. Let yourself go. If you feel like creating a particular effect, check with the music and go overboard if it is permissible. Probably you will exaggerate, but that is exactly what you want to do at this point; it is like going over every detail with a magnifying glass to make sure that you are playing correctly. By repeating the whole program day after day you will start to think in terms of the program unit instead of the composition unit. If you are a great pianist you will also develop a characteristic sound so that the music can be identified, just as a connoisseur can identify a painting by the brush strokes.

The remaining half hour of each period will be spent in slow-to-fast metronome practice of all the difficult passages in the program. Now we are overlearning, building up a margin of reserve. We are building each passage to a speed beyond that which we will need. We are practicing chord passages using our strength from slow-to-fast so that when performance calls for power we have a comfortable reserve under control.

Gradually, by dint of repetition, the exaggeration will file down, the rubati assume shape and control, extremes in dynamics and tempo will be softened, and the individual subtleties of each composer and each composition will come through, not glaringly, like headlights on a highway, but like the topography of a vast and varied landscape as seen from an airplane. The end of Phase No. 2 never comes; we advance forever.

Artur Schnabel had a detailed master plan for everything he played. He even had words to each phrase of a Schubert impromptu or a Mozart sonata. I find this a bit extreme, because I prefer to "interpret" by letting the music speak for itself; yet this was Schnabel's way of making every note fit into place. It is very important to have some general and detailed plan in mind. There are times when inspiration does not come as freely as usual; others when our instrument does not co-operate satisfactorily. I know a 'cellist who has several alternate plans of approach for every major composition on his programs, which he uses according to the weather, that is, its effect on his Stradivarius. So, even when, for some reason, we are not at our best, we can still have a solid and good performance as long as we have an architectural master plan as a lifesaver.

Now we can take a little rest, a weekend at least, completely away from music. From here on the program is yours and you've earned it. You've bought it with devotion and work and honesty to the composers. But you don't own it completely until you can give it away freely, with confidence and assurance. You must play often and be ready to play everywhere.

In *Life* magazine I saw a picture of neophyte paratroopers playing ball while they were strapped to fifty-foot poles. The legend explained that the trainees were, at first, dazzled by the height and were afraid to trust their safety belts, clinging to the poles with both arms. Playing ball, throwing it from one pole to the other, the boys had to use at least one arm, eventually both arms to throw, and so became accustomed to the feeling of height and learned to trust their safety belts. Your careful practice is your safety belt.

There is always room at the top for a great artist. There can never be enough beauty. There always are too few great personalities. The line that separates the "very good" from the "great" is slim; it is crossed by that extra effort of performance, that extra grain of imagination, that extra feeling of rapport with the audience, that extra warmth of humanity that pervades the artist's personality. With work, courage, imagination, honesty, it is within your power to enter that magic land of creative beauty. The late architect Frank Lloyd Wright said that luxury is far more important to man than necessity. We should think in terms of glamorous sound, voluptuous tone, dazzling technique, and be satisfied with nothing less. If you think on the grand scale, you will produce accordingly.

People who come to the greenroom ask me many questions. One is, "How can you play well when you have to maintain such a heavy concert schedule?" I answer that it is easier to play a season of fifty concerts than one of ten because you constantly build physical and mental stamina. It is most difficult to play only one concert a year. Constant performance keeps the polish at a high gloss and, as in baseball, continuous training gives you a high batting average. "What happens when you are not in the mood to play?" is another question. This always startles me. There can't be such a possibility. An artist does not perform by caprice. His function is to *create* a mood, a whole atmosphere for himself and his audience. Practicing makes an artist so sure-fingered that even on off-days his performance will have quality and scope, and he will be able to reach his public. I firmly believe that temperament is 90 per cent temper—that is, bad manners—and 10 per cent fear. Use the awareness of your consistent effort and the margin of reserve you have acquired to fight actively the demon of fear. If we allow it to enter our thoughts, we can be afraid to play a single piece, a small passage, even a single note. With fear it is simply a question of degree. What is the worst possible thing that can happen if you make a mistake? Your loss of reputation? Then, don't seasoned professionals who have great reputations have far greater cause for fear? Absolute perfection in art is impossible because everyone's concept is different. Who can be the judge? Whose concept is the right one? "Don't you ever make a mistake?" mothers of young pianists often ask me. Well, sometimes. We all do. No matter how hard we have worked and how well prepared we are, the public's excitement sets all the senses keenly aware and we listen and project differently from any other time. Surprising things happen, mostly caused by nerves. When you feel that you have made a slight mistake you are terrified; you lose all sense of proportion. Suddenly your memory blacks out; you clutch blindly at any straw of improvisation that will take you back to the beginning, or skip to the end or the nearest break or theme that you can remember in your frenzy. The whole thing lasts only a split second, and it feels horrible, but if we have practiced hard enough to have a high batting average it may not happen again for the next fifty concerts.

Making mistakes is almost inevitable at some stage of absorbing a certain work. I don't know of any great pianist who would not occasionally slip, and even the one I think is least liable to make mistakes is not beyond a sour note once in a while. This is not to encourage carelessness or a casual attitude toward accuracy; we must strive for maximum perfection. Yet, since we cannot skip the stage in which absorption of a work is not yet completed, since we have to go through this period of comparative instability, I wish that so many young artists were not so completely disheartened and frustrated when it happens to them. One of my colleagues—whom I consider a superb musician—is, in my opinion, handicapped in a big career only by his overanxiousness to give a flawless performance, which takes much of his spontaneous musicianship away.

Fear of critics should be no issue in performance. A critic so alert and erudite that he notices every slight slip will, by the same token, be a superior musician who will see it in proper proportion and make no issue of it if the rest of the performance is an accomplished, professional job, serious, convincing.

CHAPTER NINE

About Listening

To LISTEN IS, according to Webster, "to give an ear" or, according to Funk & Wagnall, "to heed what is heard." Listening is meaningful and conscious hearing, a special art that must be cultivated. There are many different ways in which people listen to a piece of music:

1. Most people, I believe, are first of all fascinated by the performance, and I have heard remarks like, "Did you ever see hands move so quickly?" or comments on the "fine left hand" or "brilliant octaves."

2. Other people are primarily entranced with the effect of the music. They don't pretend to know much about the technical part of playing; they have no ambitions for themselves; they go to a concert purely because they like music. They look for certain clues in the program to know what they can expect: sounds reminiscent of rippling water in a composition called *The Brook;* the association with gypsy fiddles, firelight, and dancing in Liszt's Hungarian rhapsodies. These are the people who say that they don't know music but do know what they like, and a concert either leaves them cold or carries them away completely.

3. Yet other people will compare a performance to other performances they have heard. This is almost inevitable with older people, who tend to be nostalgic for their own youthful receptiveness, and it always happens with people who have had a strong "first impression" of a composition and establish it as a yardstick.

These individual methods have limitations, however, and those limitations spell certain dangers. The ideal way to listen has something of each of them.

Intelligent listening is an art that any layman can cultivate by directing his conscious attention to all the clues: production, effect, instrumental sound, and "comparison yardstick."

Music's message reaches people in devious ways: it can appeal primarily to the emotions, or to the senses, or to the intellect. Music can change a person's mood, but the person has to be pliable and willing to co-operate. When you go to a party you can have a boring time if you sit back and do nothing, or you can have a marvelous time if you pitch in and help create for yourself, and those around you, a festive spirit. The honest listener must, first of all, learn to respond.

If we could ask Beethoven or Bach how their music should sound, we would probably be greatly surprised at their answers. Those masters did not have our instruments and could hear their music only under conditions that would not satisfy us nowadays. Sometimes, too, composers are less qualified than re-creative artists in the art of interpretation. When I played one of his works for Heitor Villa-Lobos shortly before his death, he made several suggestions I immediately carried out. Then he said, "No, play it the way you feel it, the way you think it should be done."

We all have musical concepts we develop in imagination. We identify ourselves with the performers whose ideas are bigger and better-developed versions of our own. (That is the principle on which synagogue cantors have always been chosen; their songful prayers are supposed to be the idealized embodiment of the prayers of the whole congregation.)

Those of us who are mainly interested in technique will identify themselves with a great technician whose clarity and brilliance are foremost in evidence. Those who want to be carried away by the music, regardless of production, will find their ideal in performers who re-create musical splendor, perhaps with a slight disregard for perfection.

The most important thing is to be open-minded to every kind of music. As in flying, there are invisible barriers. It was a tremendously difficult task to break the sonic barrier because it involved concepts in physics, in methods of flying, in forces never experienced. Most people have similar hidden barriers in their minds; we call them prejudices. They are man-made walls; they exist in our minds because we put them there and are very reluctant to take them down. Barriers were erected against Palestrina and Bach, against Brahms, Wagner, Debussy, Strauss, Bartók, Stravinsky—against practically any innovator.

Another mental barrier is the preconceived idea. Some

people have the notion that all Mozart must sound delicate like a pink china doll, that all Brahms must sound heavy, that all modern music is discordant. When we hear a performance that doesn't agree with our preconceived ideas we become critical, nonplused.

How many people go to a concert and wait to read the reviews the next morning to see whether they enjoyed it! How wrong! Musical taste is a very personal thing. Often you can be guided by other people's qualified judgment and stimulated to investigate further, to sharpen and educate your own feelings, but you have the last word in matters of personal preference. The greatest hope of the re-creative artist is that his study has been so thorough, his concept so honest and convincing, that he will epitomize the concepts of most of his listeners. As an audience, we should make a special effort to develop our own tastes and opinions, and not disclaim them.

It takes a great deal of receptive listening to reach the sophisticated state where *only*, say, chamber music, or contemporary music, or English madrigals, or some such special field, can satisfy a person's musical taste; in fact, when I meet such a person, I question his sincerity. First, one must try everything, from Purcell to Puccini, from Bach to Bartók. We must listen to men's choruses and harp solos, to E. Power Biggs and Vladimir Horowitz, taking in everything with an open mind. When you like something, listen to it again. There is no such thing as "good" music or "bad" music. The most popular music is that which was acclaimed by listeners who unashamedly formed their own choice. Beethoven is good box office today because people for one and a half centuries have enjoyed his music enough to want to come back for more. Regardless of whether, in your musical taste, you become a conformist or non-conformist, a faddist, or a conservative, be candid. There is the Hans Christian Andersen story about the emperor's new clothes that supposedly only the very wise could see, until a child innocently pointed and said, "Look! The emperor has no clothes on at all!"

Choose honestly the things you like best, enjoy them, learn about them and their composers, analyze them from the viewpoint of performance and its effect on you, and be proud of developing your own good individual taste. You can have a lot of fun by turning on the radio and trying to identify the music that happens to be playing. There are plenty of musical clues. First try to identify the period: is it classic, romantic, impressionist, contemporary? Does it have themes or rhythms that seem indigenous to a particular country? Do the melodic or harmonic styles remind you of another composer's works? See how close you can come by guessing.

You will find that, as you develop into an analytical listener and discover new sound colors, your musical taste will become broader and different. If you don't like Bartók today, give him another chance next week, next month, next year. Human nature is afraid of the unfamiliar, and most great masters had to run the gantlet of hesitancy, criticism, even hostility. One of Mozart's string quintets was returned by a publisher who felt that the copyist must have made a mistake; Mozart couldn't possibly write such dissonances. Wagner had to build his own theater to realize his potential and was almost sixty when he struck it rich. Beethoven was patted on the shoulder by some critics and told to improve his style by listening to the music of some third-rate salon composer. Richard Strauss and Stravinsky provoked riots in the concert hall. It is impossible to know whose music will be heard in a hundred years and whose will be forgotten. But we can, and should, champion our choice of today. The false fear of saying the wrong thing makes many of us with valid and authoritative opinions retreat to platitudes and generalities. What is the point in being merely tolerant? No one, and certainly not an artist, wants to be merely tolerated. Artists need encouragement, acceptance, constructive criticism.

The words "mature" and "immature" are being abused to a degree that invites discussion. Webster's dictionary defines "immature" as "unripe, not arrived at full development." A fruit slowly ripens in the sun all spring to achieve a brief period of maturity, then, if not picked, it becomes overripe, deteriorates, and spoils. The work of an artist mellows, develops, and matures all through his life. Full maturity would imply perfection, the peak, but as we perfect ourselves we constantly discover new areas to explore. An artist's whole life span is taken up with the maturing process; in this sense, he can never hope to reach absolute maturity.

Not every artist, however, will admit this fact. It takes a certain amount of humility. One of the humblest people I have ever met is Mischa Elman, despite the many stories that circulate about his vanity. Once a gushing lady addressed him in the greenroom and swooned: "Mr. Elman, you are a god." Elman, sharp-witted as always, replied, "No, madam, a god doesn't improve, but I do."

In art, as in life, the Why and the How are often more significant than the What. If we try to understand why a certain artist deviated from the traditional pattern, and if his playing can convince us from his point of view, then we might just as well accept it on its own terms even though we disagree.

The vast American public stayed away in droves from Rubinstein and Gieseking when they were in their artistic prime. Rachmaninoff and Harold Bauer knew the bitterness of critical condemnation. Think of how many more years we and they could have brought enjoyment to each other had we but listened to their art instead of waiting until a lifetime of hard work earned them sufficient reputation to bring forth the applauding public. Let's not make the same old mistake over and over again; let's not wait for artistic merit to find us. By developing our own musical taste and having confidence in our own judgment we can rejoice in our own discoveries and champion the artists of today, the proud heritage of tomorrow.

CHAPTER TEN

From My Teaching Experience

MUSIC CAN BE taken up at any time. A good teacher will use as many different approaches to instruction as he has students, for no two individuals are alike. A grandmother can find tremendous pleasure in studying the piano (it is healthy for her fingers, too). A businessman will find piano practice a great nerve soother and will get a real thrill of accomplishment from producing attractive melodies through his own efforts. The slogan of the Orchestre Symphonique de Paris is: "One can live without music but not as well!"

If a child grows up in a home where music is a part of everyday living, he will subconsciously develop a broad musical taste even before he ever attends a concert. He does not have to sit in reverence during an entire radio or phonograph reproduction of a classic; enjoying music should not be a chore but a pleasure. When the child attends his first live performance it will be a revelation to him to watch music "come to life."

The most important things a music teacher can give to a student are a healthy and realistic attitude toward music, good piano manners, a feeling of security at the keyboard, and the ability to sight-read pleasurably. With these assets the student can look forward to reaching musical independence; he will be able to come back to his music at any time and go on without a teacher if need be. If he manages also to acquire the ability to play "show pieces," they should be regarded as dividends rather than the net result of his music lessons.

The main thing is that the beginner has faith in his teacher and stays with him only if he trusts him implicitly. Studies in the psychology of learning show us that if we plot learning ability on a graph it will be shaped like a giant S—periods of progress will alternate with plateau periods that will seem comparatively fallow. During such periods we will need confidence in our teacher and in our objectives.

Teachers can help a student enormously by writing down the next lesson's assignment and telling him clearly what his daily preparation for that goal should be. For instance:

> Play C-major, A-minor, G-major, and E-minor scales and arpeggios both hands together, with the metronome at sixty, at four notes to the beat.
> Read a Burgmüller study *carefully* every day.
> Learn the first section of the assigned Bach invention by playing it six times with each hand every day, paying special attention to phrase and dynamic markings. Lift left hand for rests.

Play a Schubert waltz, as if in a concert, twice at the
end of each practice period.

Review Bartók dance. Make an exercise of the mordents in the right hand.

Read Chapter No.—— from Ethel Peyser's *How Music
Grew*.

This indicates clearly what the pupil is expected to
accomplish in his practice period. It reminds him of important points that might slip his mind. Also, over a period
of time, parents, teacher, the pupil himself, can follow his
development and see which material was covered and
which practice methods were used. Clara Schumann's father, who was her teacher, had her keep a musical diary,
which she kept nearly as long as she lived. Many youngsters who "don't want to practice" really don't know *what*
to practice or how. Parents can co-operate by monitoring
the work from time to time, offering praise and encouragement, and assigning a definite unalterable period every day as Practice Time. An hour per day is the absolute
minimum that cannot be replaced by, say, a three-hour
session twice a week. The mechanics of playing require the
physical drill of constant repetition. A well-planned and
well-balanced study program will give optimum results
even with a pupil of limited time and talent. The child will
accept this discipline and enjoy it, even though he may
occasionally grumble—as we all do sometimes at everyday
chores.

Further, to accustom the student to communicating
the music he has learned, the good teacher holds informal

class meetings periodically—about once a month—where students can listen to each other, discuss repertoire, and enjoy the experience of performance. For special occasions, such as a composer's birthday, student's could be encouraged to practice a particular segment of their repertoire; how about a Beethoven Festival, or an Evening of Contemporary Music? A book report by at least one pupil on a teacher-selected music book should be read at each gathering; perhaps a prize could be given to the best report on the assigned book. Artists constantly learn new works to fill new programs; pupils do the same, even if their "concerts" are only in the teacher's studio. Artists' performances improve with every concert; teachers should create opportunities for all their pupils to perform as often as possible. Theodor Leschetizky used to invite all his pupils to bring their music on an appointed evening; the music was placed on a table and the master selected one piece at random that was played by the student who had brought it. A conscientious teacher will find many ways to stimulate a pupil.

POSTURE AND HAND POSITION

Begin by learning good habits at the keyboard. The easiest way is often the best; relaxation and alertness are necessary to all physical effort. Sit comfortably but straight, shoulders down but not hunched, elbows in, arms hanging level with the keyboard, wrists somewhat higher so that the hands hang slightly when the fingers push down the keys. One of my earliest teachers, a Leschetizky pupil, called this high-wrist position a "Roman Arch." (See end paper illustration.) This suspension of the hand from the wrist causes the tone to be controlled by the weight given to each individual finger when pressing down the key. This weight touch gives us relaxed control in all finger technique and production of tone. Solid, firm fingers are the foundation of a good finger technique; each finger must be well raised and firmly put down so that every key touches the bottom. Sit with your backbone ramrod-straight. When you play at either end of the keyboard your whole body moves in that direction so that the body's strength can support the hands. Anton Rubinstein obtained his famous power by leaning the whole trunk of his body forward, backbone still ramrod-straight, to add its weight to a chord. Artur Schnabel used to lean back to give the hands a floating feeling during a cantilena phrase.

LEARNING NOTES AND RHYTHM

A very young beginner can learn to find C by establishing that it is immediately to the left of the two black keys. He can make a game of finding C all the way up and down the keyboard. Then he finds CD, CDE, and we are off to a good start in learning the names of all the white keys. To teach the concept of sharps and flats, explain that the smallest possible interval on the piano is called a half step. A half step to the right, whether the key is white or black, takes the name "sharp." A half step to the left, whether the key is white or black, takes the name "flat." The same process takes place with the concepts of whole step. In this way the beginner gets an accurate and healthy way of thinking about sharps and flats on the piano, and also an introduction to rudimentary harmony through his early familiarity with intervals.

COUNTING

When the beginner learns to count, help him to understand the digits as a horizontal reading concept rather than a variation of arithmetic lessons that the child associates with vertical lines. Use "and" freely—"1 and 2 and 3 and 4 and . . ." For triplets say "1-and-and, 2-and-and, 3-and-and, 4-and-and." For sixteenths say "1-i-an-i, 2-i-an-i, 3-i-an-i, 4-i-an-i." Dotted notes will not be a problem if the teacher writes the proper counting numerals and syllables from left to right on the student's music until he understands the new concept. While the pupil is perfecting this new skill, he should count every new piece through, away from the keyboard, until he can hear the composition correctly with his inner ear.

SOLFÈGE

In Europe solfège, the art of verbalizing music, was considered for centuries an essential part of every student's training. It is presumed to be an invaluable aid in reading and memorizing. It takes quite a bit of practice to become adept at saying out loud all the Italian syllables (do, re, mi, etc.) to the notes of a Bach prelude up to speed. The underlying purpose of getting the music into your consciousness is a good one. It seems to me, however, that many of the best solfège students become so mechanical in this skill that it loses its value, and I merely suggest it as an extra aid when necessary. For example, in learning an intricate finger passage the fingers may learn more rapidly than the brain, and the memory may fail to retain every note; in such a case the student will mentally review the problem and use solfège to learn more thoroughly.

HARMONY

The study of elementary harmony is of vital importance to every talented music student. The mind and the ear must recognize intervals, both melodically and harmonically. Harmony will also teach someone who has "no ear for music" to recognize the basic mathematical laws of symmetry that are the skeleton of all composition. If a student has learned the basic harmonic pattern of a major scale and can transpose it in his mind as well as with his fingers, he will not balk at reading compositions containing a number of sharps and flats in the signature. The study of harmony will get the mind accustomed to directing the fingers at all times; using the inner ear, the mind will memorize harmonically, and that knowledge will enable us to form a clearer mental picture of the composition's architecture. The study of harmony is a lifetime's chore. After the student acquires a basic introductory knowledge, he and his teacher can decide whether to continue and take up counterpoint and composition. Just as the study of Latin is valuable to the specialist in Romance languages, elementary harmony is an essential part of a gifted pianist's early training. The teacher can choose from many available manuals the method that proceeds according to the needs of the individual student, and assign lessons that he can absorb most easily.

SCALES AND ARPEGGIOS

It takes years to acquire real hand familiarity with the keyboard. During this time there should be daily practice sessions featuring a definitely planned program of scales. Most of the music of Western civilization is built from the basic tones of one or several of the twenty-four major and minor scales. To have a complete hand knowledge of them is essential, and a sensible investment for future freedom from technical fear. The standard best fingerings for major, minor, chromatic scales, and arpeggios have long since been established, and these fingerings seem most comfortable for all hands, regardless of size. The imaginative teacher will find stimulating ways in which to make scales and arpeggios interesting. Some technical material should be practiced as routine as the warm-up before every study period. The muscles become loosened and accustomed to the movements and will function automatically when the need arises. Dexterity that can be taken for granted is the most valuable tool of which musical imagination can make use. It means freedom. So often nervousness, or a piano's light action, or just plain exuberance will cause us to take an unusually fast tempo that will tax our powers of concentration to the limit. We have to know that our hands are trained so that we can rely on them to carry the passage, whatever the circumstances.

Scales and arpeggios in all the major and minor keys,

and the chromatic scale in four octaves up and down the keyboard, are an absolute necessity. We are not going to write them all out here because it is easy to acquire a manual that lists them all correctly and with accurate fingering. The teacher and student can have a lot of fun devising ways of practicing these essentials:

Hands separately.

Hands together at intervals of a third, sixth, octave, or tenth.

Cross hands (both ways), particularly useful in promoting independent action of both hands playing together.

Staccato (finger, wrist, from the elbow).

Forte in one hand, piano in the other.

Legato in one hand, staccato in the other.

Different rhythms and accents, as indicated on P. 38.

With the metronome slow to fast.

Both harmonic and melodic minor modes should be studied in all the tonalities. Dominant-seventh arpeggios in all positions are extremely useful after the student has learned all the scales. Establish new harmonic sequences every day. Examples:

C major, C minor, dominant seventh starting on C (C Eb Gb Ab), leading to Db major, and so on, until you complete the circle.

C major, C minor, dominant seventh starting on D
(D F♯ A C), leading to G major, and so on, until you
complete the circle.

C major, C minor, dominant seventh starting on C
(C E G B♭), leading to F major, and so on, until you
complete the cycle.

To make up good sequences is good practice.

Two problems often beset the beginner learning the
scales and arpeggios: (1) moving the thumb under the
hand quickly and smoothly, without moving elbow and
arm; (2) moving the hand over the thumb without jerking
the elbow.

Here are some ways to avoid these mistakes: blocking
scales and arpeggios.

Examples of a "blocked" scale and arpeggio. Let your thumb do
all the work!

Solving the "thumb-underneath" problem is of particular importance, and if you don't seem to need special exercise at first, you may need it later when you work with the metronome to acquire speed. Keep your shoulders down.

FINGERING

Here is our favorite fingering for the chromatic scale:

> ascending C to C, right hand 2313123123412
> left hand 1313214321321

> descending, right hand 2143213213132
> left hand 1231234123131

We suggest this because the 1 2 3 4 gives added smoothness in speed by giving the thumb a rest. We don't recommend the two-octave chromatic scale fingering that seemingly follows the same smoothness and rest-the-thumb principle, because it accustoms the hand to a two-octave sequence, and most chromatic scales in compositions are not so long. The one-octave sequence is simpler for the hand to memorize, and more practical. It is also important to learn the chromatic scale in the three back fingers, particularly in the right hand, but also in the left.

> ascending C to C, right hand 5343453434345
> left hand 4343543434354

> descending, right hand 5434343543435
> left hand 4534343453434

When you are ready for the chromatic scale in minor thirds, here is the best fingering, derived from Busoni:

ascending, thumb on C 3453434345343
1212212121221

descending, 2nd finger on C 3435434343543
2121212212122

This is applicable to major thirds and fourths as well. The sliding second finger ensures a smooth legato line, both ascending and descending, A chromatic scale in thirds is not easy to master. It is a veritable hurdle, takes a long time and a lot of patience, but it is a proud accomplishment. Use every device: developers, accented rhythms, metronome slow to fast.

As I have a small hand, I find that the best fingering for chromatic scales in sixths and octaves is the combination of the three back fingers, as above, and jumping thumb. It may be that a larger hand will find something more suitable. In any case, turn your wrists toward your body so that your hands are pointed in the right direction.

Fingering is a very personal matter: what is best for one pianist need not necessarily be best for another. The important thing is for every pianist to have basic, automatic fingering patterns that will be the solid foundation of a sure finger technique. The only way to establish them is to be consistent during practice sessions. Only in this way can we be sure of our kinesthetic response. If perchance during a performance, some minute accident occurs that "derails" the fingers temporarily, the mind will bring the hands back to their whole pattern immediately. Having a fingering pattern firmly established in the first place is the best insurance against being "derailed"; moreover, if the pattern habit is established firmly enough, it will take very strong jarring to upset kinesthetic response.

SIGHT READING

Learning to become a good reader can be a simple, most enjoyable occupation. You should always improve reading technique; even concertizing artists continue to work on it. It is imperative right from the start to learn to read without looking at the keyboard, similar to the touch system in typing. There is a tremendous fund of good reading material from which to choose. For the early beginner I recommend Burgmüller studies, Bertini études, duet arrangements of folk tunes. However, these exercises are not of sufficient permanent value to merit the complete process of learning and memorizing that will be required in mastering miniature compositions by Mozart, Bach, Handel, Haydn, Purcell, and the like. Duet reading material is particularly helpful in developing a good sense of rhythm. Eventually, reading something every day, the student should go through all the Haydn and Mozart sonatas, the Haydn and Mozart symphonies (in four-hand arrangement), Handel sonatas for violin and piano, etc. The literature is infinite, and curiosity is the best guide.

Learn early that music is a thrilling group activity. To be an accompanist is a special art and teaches you teamwork. Accompany a chorus or string ensemble, solo violin, vocal selections from light operas, and you will learn to blend and mold your own tone. Play chamber music and try to inspire your partners with beautiful sound and rhythmic pulse. It is also the best preparation for concerti. The experience of co-operation, of melodic and rhythmic rapport with other musicians, of listening to others as well as yourself, of making adjustments and allowances while keeping up your own responsibilities—all of the many elements in piano-orchestra relations can be learned in chamber music in a most pleasurable way.

Reading well means to read *everything in the score*. Reading is the first step in learning a new composition and it is of paramount importance to read so completely that no mistake will be learned. Correct notes and rhythm, rests, tempo and dynamic markings, legato slurs and phrasing; the ability to keep the eyes ahead of the hands, of noticing scale and arpeggio patterns so that fingering will be smooth: all these skills can only be acquired by the daily reading of music throughout your musical life.

CONCLUSION

THE RE-CREATIVE ARTIST must eagerly participate in life's challenges and experiences in order to record them in his subconscious. He must live fully and courageously, accepting and giving with a full heart so that he may become tempered with wisdom. He must absorb the greatest in literature; the visual arts of painting, sculpture, and architecture; the re-creative arts of dancing, acting, and music, to be able to give of himself lavishly, generously.

B-47

$2.99

Music at your Fingertips

by Ruth Slenczynska

with the collaboration of
Ann M. Lingg

Written by one of America's most brilliant artists, MUSIC AT YOUR FINGERTIPS is a valuable, practical book covering many aspects of the technique required in piano practicing and performing. It is written for the beginner and the serious student, the teacher and the listener as well.

Miss Slenczynska's profound understanding of her profession is passed on to the reader in a clear and forceful manner. She carefully examines the necessary personality factors, physical strengths, and the imaginative and interpretative powers of the individual in relation to the piano. She covers every major aspect of technique including fingering, pedaling, hand positions, legato and staccato, counting and memorizing—bringing the experience of her more than thirty years of professional performing to the aspiring artist and to the concertgoing public.

A notable feature of MUSIC AT YOUR FINGERTIPS is its attention to the art of

(continued on back flap)

"Whe
octav
open
Men
*Conc
into ¡
call i
curle
be ou